The IGAP Coach

Coach

GRADE 6
MATHEMATICS

by Jerome D. Kaplan, Ed.D.

EDUCATIONAL DESIGN, INC.   EDI 228

ISBN# 0-87694-512-4   EDI 228

TABLE OF CONTENTS

INTRODUCTION: To the Student

This book is called **The IGAP Coach**. It will help you prepare for the Illinois Grade 6 IGAP (Illinois Goal Assessment Program) Test in Math.

The IGAP Coach will help you in these ways:

- It shows you what the math questions on the IGAP test are like.
- It tells you what you need to know in order to do well on the test.
- Finally, it gives you practice with the math that is important for the test.

Here is some useful information about the test:

1. The test is given in early March.
2. The test consists of 70 questions.
3. All questions are multiple choice. You pick the one correct answer from 5 options.
4. The test is given in two sessions of 40 minutes each.
5. No points are deducted if you get a wrong answer.
6. You may bring a calculator to the test, but check with your school to make sure you bring the correct calculator.
7. The test covers these mathematics topics:
   - Computation
   - Ratios and Percentages
   - Measurement
   - Algebra
   - Geometry
   - Data Collection and Analysis
   - Estimation

Each lesson of this book has three sections:

- *Step-by-step ways to find the answers to questions* just like those on the test
- *Examples* worked out so that you get a good picture of what you need to know
- *A Practice Section* that gives you a chance to check the skills of the lesson

The Practice Section allows you to see if you can really do the questions on the test. Make sure you do all the questions in this section.

At the end of the book, Lesson 34 gives you *Test-Taking Tips* about how to take the IGAP Math test. You should use these tips when you take the *Practice Test* at the end of the book.

Good luck!

LESSON 1 COMPUTATION: Word Names for Numbers

These examples will help you read and write numbers.

Example 1: How do you read the number **385,873**?

Step 1. If there is **one comma**, then the number **in front of the comma** tells you how many **thousands**:

385 is in front of the comma, so we start by saying—

"Three hundred eighty-five thousand . . ."

Step 2. Complete the number name by saying the number after the comma:

"Three hundred eighty-five thousand . . .

" . . . eight hundred seventy-three."

Example 2: How do you say **4,528,601**?

If there are **two commas**, then the number **in front of the first comma** tells you how many **millions**:

4 stands for four million. The complete number is:

"Four million,

five hundred twenty-eight thousand,

six hundred one."

PRACTICE

Write the word name for these numbers.

1. 3,840 _____

2. 71,200 _____

3. 451,839 _____

4. 6,000,000 _____

5. 2,809,500 _____

How do you say the number? Choose the correct word name for each.

6. 4,500

    A. four hundred thousand, five hundred

    B. five hundred thousand, four hundred

    C. four thousand, five hundred

    D. four thousand, fifty

    E. four thousand, five

7. 762,800

    A. seven hundred sixty-two thousand

    B. seven hundred sixty-two thousand, eight hundred

    C. seven hundred sixty-two thousand, eighty

    D. six hundred seventy-two thousand, eight hundred

    E. seven hundred sixty-two thousand, eighty hundred

8. 9,400,000

    A. nine million, four hundred

    B. nine thousand, four hundred

    C. nine thousand, forty thousand

    D. nine million, forty thousand

    E. nine million, four hundred thousand

9. 2,405,700

    A. two million, four hundred five thousand, seven hundred

    B. two million, four hundred fifty thousand, seven hundred

    C. two million, four hundred five thousand

    D. two million, four hundred five thousand, seventy

    E. two million, forty-five thousand, seven hundred

10. 8,004,650

    A. eight million, four thousand, six hundred

    B. eight million, forty thousand, six hundred fifty

    C. eight million, four thousand, six hundred fifty

    D. eight million, four hundred thousand, six hundred fifty

    E. eight million, four thousand, sixty-five

LESSON 2 COMPUTATION: Simplifying Fractions: Lowest Terms; Changing a Mixed Number to an Improper Fraction

1. Lowest Terms

To simplify a fraction, write it in lowest terms.

Example 1: Reduce $\frac{15}{45}$ to lowest terms.

> **Step 1.** Find the greatest number that divides both 15 and 45.
>
> 3 divides both 15 and 45. So does 5. But the <u>greatest</u>
>
> number that divides both 15 and 45 is **15**.
>
> **Step 2.** Divide both numerator and denominator by the number you found in Step 1.
>
> $$\frac{15 \div \mathbf{15}}{45 \div \mathbf{15}} = \frac{1}{3}$$
>
> $\frac{15}{45}$ simplified to lowest terms is $\frac{1}{3}$.

Example 2: Reduce $\frac{24}{30}$ to lowest terms.

> The greatest number that divides both 24 and 30 is 6. So,
>
> $$\frac{24 \div \mathbf{6}}{30 \div \mathbf{6}} = \frac{4}{5}$$
>
> So $\frac{24}{30}$ in lowest terms is $\frac{4}{5}$.

Example 3: Reduce $\frac{16}{35}$ to lowest terms.

> There is no number (other than 1) that divides both 16 and 35. So $\frac{16}{35}$ is already in lowest terms. It is already simplified.

2. Changing a Mixed Number to an Improper Fraction

A **_mixed number_** is made up of **_a whole number and a fraction_**. For example:

$$1\frac{2}{3} \qquad 7\frac{1}{6} \qquad 12\frac{4}{7}$$

An **improper fraction** is a **fraction greater than 1**. You can always tell an improper fraction because the **numerator is greater than the denominator**. These are improper fractions:

$$\frac{5}{2} \qquad \frac{7}{6} \qquad \frac{9}{4}$$

Example 1: Change $7\frac{3}{4}$ to an improper fraction.

To change a mixed number to an improper fraction, we use all parts of the mixed number.

Step 1. Multiply the denominator (4) by the whole number (7):

$$7 \overleftarrow{} x \underleftarrow{} \frac{3}{4}$$

Multiply: 4 x 7 = 28

Step 2. Add the numerator (3) of the original fraction to 28:

$$7 \overleftarrow{} \overset{+ \to 3}{\underset{x \to 4}{}}$$

Add: 28 + 3 = 31

Step 3. Form a fraction with 31 as the numerator and with 4 as the denominator. (4 is the original denominator of $7\frac{3}{4}$.)

The fraction is $\frac{31}{4}$. It is an improper fraction.

$$7\frac{3}{4} = \frac{31}{4}$$

Example 2: Change $2\frac{9}{25}$ to an improper fraction.

Multiply: 25 x 2 = 50

Add: 50 + 9 = 59

Form the improper fraction: $\frac{59}{25}$

$$2\frac{9}{25} = \frac{59}{25}$$

PRACTICE

Reduce each fraction to lowest terms.

1. $\dfrac{4}{6}$ = _____

2. $\dfrac{21}{35}$ = _____

3. $\dfrac{20}{30}$ = _____

4. $\dfrac{24}{28}$ = _____

Change each mixed number to an improper fraction.

5. $1\dfrac{1}{2}$ = _____

6. $4\dfrac{1}{6}$ = _____

7. $3\dfrac{2}{3}$ = _____

8. $10\dfrac{3}{4}$ = _____

9. $6\dfrac{3}{10}$ = _____

10. $8\dfrac{5}{8}$ = _____

11. $20\dfrac{5}{6}$ = _____

Choose the correct answer for each of the following.

12. Change $4\dfrac{5}{8}$ to an improper fraction.

    A. $\dfrac{37}{5}$

    B. $\dfrac{28}{5}$

    C. $\dfrac{44}{8}$

    D. $\dfrac{32}{8}$

    E. $\dfrac{37}{8}$

13. What is another way to write $\dfrac{2}{5} \times 2\dfrac{1}{4}$?

    A. $\dfrac{2}{5} \times \dfrac{7}{4}$

    B. $\dfrac{2}{5} \times \dfrac{8}{4}$

    C. $\dfrac{2}{5} \times \dfrac{9}{2}$

    D. $\dfrac{2}{5} \times \dfrac{9}{4}$

    E. $\dfrac{2}{5} \times \dfrac{8}{4}$

14. Change $3\dfrac{5}{6}$ to an improper fraction.

    A. $\dfrac{18}{6}$

    B. $\dfrac{33}{6}$

    C. $\dfrac{28}{6}$

    D. $\dfrac{23}{6}$

    E. $\dfrac{24}{6}$

15. What is another way to write $\dfrac{7}{8} + 4\dfrac{3}{4}$?

    A. $\dfrac{7}{8} + \dfrac{19}{3}$

    B. $\dfrac{7}{8} + \dfrac{19}{4}$

    C. $\dfrac{7}{8} + \dfrac{16}{3}$

    D. $\dfrac{7}{8} + \dfrac{16}{4}$

    E. $\dfrac{7}{8} + \dfrac{12}{4}$

LESSON 3 COMPUTATION:
Finding the Fraction of a Whole Number

There are two ways you can find a fraction of a whole number.

1. First way: *By dividing into equal groups.*

> **Example 1:** Jamie has 12 computer disks. If one-third of them are games, how many are games?
>
> To solve this problem, find $\frac{1}{3}$ of 12.

> **Step 1.** Since the fraction is $\frac{1}{3}$, divide the disks into 3 equal groups.

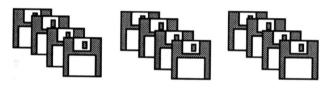

> **Step 2.** Count the number in each group:
>
> Each group has 4 disks in it.
>
> $$\frac{1}{3} \text{ of 12 is 4.}$$
>
> There are 4 disks that are games.

> **Example 2:** Find $\frac{1}{2}$ of 10.
>
> Divide 10 into 2 equal groups.

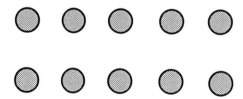

> There are 5 in each group.
> $\frac{1}{2}$ of 10 = 5

2. **Second way:** *By dividing the whole number by the denominator.*

Here is a more direct way to find the fraction of a whole number. If the numerator of the fraction is 1 (such as $\frac{1}{2}$, $\frac{1}{3}$, and $\frac{1}{4}$), then all you have to do is:

Divide the whole number by the denominator of the fraction.

Example 1: Find $\frac{1}{4}$ of 24.

Divide: $24 \div 4 = 6$

$\frac{1}{4}$ of $24 = 6$

Example 2: Mabel has 30 phone calls to make. She will make $\frac{1}{6}$ of them in the morning. How many will she make in the morning?

To solve this problem, find $\frac{1}{6}$ of 30.

Divide: $30 \div 6 = 5$

Mabel will make 5 phone calls in the morning.

PRACTICE

1. $\frac{1}{4}$ of 24 = _____

2. $\frac{1}{3}$ of 36 = _____

3. $\frac{1}{7}$ of 49 = _____

4. $\frac{1}{6}$ of 60 = _____

5. $\frac{1}{10}$ of 200 = _____

Choose the correct answers.

6. There are 25 students in Bonnie's class. If one-fifth of them walk to school, how many walk to school?

    A. 20

    B. 15

    C. 10

    D. 5

    E. 1

7. Find $\frac{1}{3}$ of 12.

    A. 3

    B. 4

    C. 6

    D. 8

    E. 10

8. What is $\frac{1}{9}$ of 27?

    A. 3

    B. 4

    C. 5

    D. 6

    E. 9

9. Rashan watched 35 hours of TV last week. One-seventh of the time he watched comedy shows. How many hours did he watch comedy shows?

    A. 4

    B. 5

    C. 6

    D. 7

    E. 8

10. Juana said that $\frac{1}{5}$ of the 400 pounds of paper that her class collected can be recycled. How many pounds can be recycled?

    A. 20

    B. 40

    C. 50

    D. 60

    E. 80

11. If one-fourth of the squares shown below are taken away, how many will be left?

    A. 2

    B. 3

    C. 4

    D. 5

    E. 6

LESSON 4 COMPUTATION:
Changing Fractions to Decimals and Finding the Smallest or Largest Fraction

1. Changing Fractions to Decimals

Example 1: Change $\frac{2}{5}$ to a decimal.

$\frac{2}{5}$ means 2 divided by 5, so do the math:

$$5)\overline{\begin{smallmatrix}0.4\\2.0\end{smallmatrix}}$$

$\frac{2}{5}$ = 0.4

You can always find the decimal for a fraction by dividing the numerator by the denominator. It is still a good idea to memorize the most common conversions from fractions to decimals.

$\frac{1}{2}$ 0.5	$\frac{1}{8}$ 0.125
	$\frac{3}{8}$ 0.375
$\frac{1}{3}$ . . . . 0.333... or 0.33	$\frac{5}{8}$ 0.625
$\frac{2}{3}$ . . . . 0.666... or 0.67	$\frac{7}{8}$ 0.875
$\frac{1}{4}$ 0.25	$\frac{1}{10}$ 0.2
$\frac{3}{4}$ 0.75	$\frac{3}{10}$ 0.3
	$\frac{7}{10}$ 0.7
$\frac{1}{5}$ 0.2	$\frac{9}{10}$ 0.9
$\frac{2}{5}$ 0.4	
$\frac{3}{5}$ 0.6	
$\frac{4}{5}$ 0.8	

You will find some "gaps" in the lists. For example, $\frac{2}{8}$ is not listed, since it is equivalent to $\frac{1}{4}$, which <u>is</u> listed.

2. Finding the Smallest or Largest Fraction

Example 1: Which of these fractions is the smallest: $\frac{2}{3}$, $\frac{3}{4}$, $\frac{3}{8}$, $\frac{7}{10}$ or $\frac{13}{16}$?

Here are two ways to find the smallest fraction. (The same methods apply to finding the largest fraction.)

Method 1. *Use the Table on p. 9—change fractions to decimals.*

Use the table to write fractions as decimals:

$$\frac{2}{3} = 0.67$$

$$\frac{3}{4} = 0.75$$

$$\frac{3}{8} = 0.375$$

$$\frac{7}{10} = 0.7$$

Since $\frac{13}{16}$ is not in the table, divide:

$$16 \overline{)13.0000} \quad 0.8125$$

$$\frac{13}{16} = 0.8125$$

Compare all the decimals.

The smallest decimal is 0.375, so the smallest fraction is $\frac{3}{8}$.

Method 2. *Estimate the size of the fractions.*

Divide the fractions into those that are greater than $\frac{1}{2}$ and those that are less than $\frac{1}{2}$. Use this rule:

A fraction is greater than $\frac{1}{2}$ if the numerator is more than half of the denominator.

For example, $\frac{3}{6}$ is equal to $\frac{1}{2}$ (3 is half of 6). So $\frac{4}{6}$ is greater than $\frac{1}{2}$, and $\frac{2}{6}$ is less than $\frac{1}{2}$.

In the problem:

fractions greater than $\frac{1}{2}$: $\frac{2}{3}$, $\frac{3}{4}$, $\frac{7}{10}$ and $\frac{13}{16}$

fractions less than $\frac{1}{2}$: $\frac{3}{8}$

$\frac{3}{8}$ is the only fraction less than $\frac{1}{2}$, so it is the smallest fraction.

PRACTICE

Change each of these fractions to decimals.

1. $\dfrac{1}{2}$ = _____

2. $\dfrac{3}{4}$ = _____

3. $\dfrac{37}{100}$ = _____

4. $\dfrac{256}{1000}$ = _____

5. $\dfrac{3}{10}$ = _____

6. $\dfrac{5}{16}$ = _____

Choose the correct answer for each of the following.

7. Which fraction is the largest?

   A. $\dfrac{1}{5}$

   B. $\dfrac{3}{10}$

   C. $\dfrac{3}{8}$

   D. $\dfrac{5}{6}$

   E. $\dfrac{1}{4}$

8. Which fraction is the smallest?

   A. $\dfrac{2}{3}$

   B. $\dfrac{4}{5}$

   C. $\dfrac{11}{16}$

   D. $\dfrac{3}{8}$

   E. $\dfrac{1}{2}$

9. Choose the decimal for $\dfrac{7}{8}$.

   A. 0.375

   B. 0.5

   C. 0.6

   D. 0.625

   E. 0.875

10. Choose the decimal for $\dfrac{3}{5}$.

   A. 0.6

   B. 0.06

   C. 0.5

   D. 0.8

   E. 1.4

LESSON 5 COMPUTATION:
Exponents

Mathematics is full of abbreviations. A special abbreviation is used when we show repeated multiplication. For example, instead of writing

$$6 \times 6 \times 6 \times 6$$

we write

$$6^4$$

The raised number ^{4} stands for the number of times we multiply by 6.
It is called the **exponent** of 6.
We read 6^4 as "6 to the fourth power," or "6 to the fourth."
Since $6 \times 6 \times 6 \times 6 = 1296$, we write

$$6^4 = 1296$$

and say "6 to the fourth equals 1296."

When the exponents are 2 and 3, we usually say something different.
    If the exponent is 2, as in 5^2, we say "5 squared""instead of "5 to the second."
    If the exponent is 3, as in 4^3, we say "4 cubed" instead of "4 to the third."

When you do not see an exponent, then you know it is 1:
$$7 = 7^1$$

Example 1: Find the value for 5^4.
        5^4 stands for 5 to the fourth, or
            $$5 \times 5 \times 5 \times 5$$
        $$5 \times 5 \times 5 \times 5 = 625$$

Example 2: What number does 14 squared stand for?
        14 squared is the same as 14^2 .
        14^2 means 14×14 .
        $$14 \times 14 = 196$$

PRACTICE

Find the value for each of the following.

1. 6 cubed   _____

2. 12 squared   _____

3. 3^5 _____

4. 7^2 _____

5. 2^6 _____

6. 10^3 _____

Choose the correct answer for each.

7. What is 5 x 5 x 5 in exponential form?

     A. 3^5

     B. 125

     C. 25

     D. 5^3

     E. 15

8. What is 2 x 2 x 2 x 2 in exponential form?

     A. 2^5

     B. 2^4

     C. 8

     D. 16

     E. 32

9. Find the value of 10 squared.

     A. 10

     B. 20

     C. 50

     D. 100

     E. 1000

10. Find the value of 8^2.

     A. 8

     B. 16

     C. 32

     D. 48

     E. 64

11. Find the value of 7 cubed.

     A. 777

     B. 729

     C. 343

     D. 77

     E. 49

12. Find the value of 10^4.

     A. 10

     B. 100

     C. 1000

     D. 10,000

     E. 100,000

LESSON 6 RATIOS AND PERCENTAGES: Writing Ratios and Proportions

1. Ratios

A ratio compares two numbers. A ratio is usually written as a fraction.

Example 1: Jack's team has 20 players and Bill's team has 15. What is the ratio of the number of players on Jack's team to the number of players on Bill's team?

    Step 1. Compare the numbers by writing a fraction.

        The first number is the numerator and the second number is the denominator: $\frac{20}{15}$

    Step 2. Reduce the fraction to lowest terms:
$$\frac{20}{15} = \frac{4}{3}$$

Say this ratio as "4 to 3". (Another way to write a ratio is to use the colon symbol. Instead of $\frac{4}{3}$ you can write 4 : 3.)

Note: If the ratio is an improper fraction, do **NOT** change it to a mixed number.

Example 2: Teresa has 12 ideas for a class trip and Manny has 15 ideas. What is the ratio of the number of ideas Teresa has to the number Manny has?

    Write a fraction: $\frac{12}{15}$

    Reduce the fraction: $\frac{12}{15} = \frac{4}{5}$

    The ratio is 4 to 5.

Example 3: Fifty students in the sixth grade say their favorite subject is science, while 25 students say that math is their favorite subject. What is the ratio of the number of students choosing science to those choosing math?

    Write a fraction: $\frac{50}{25}$

    Reduce the fraction: $\frac{50}{25} = 2$

    Write the whole number 2 as a fraction: $\frac{2}{1}$

    The ratio is 2 to 1.

Note: If a ratio reduces to a whole number, write the whole number as a fraction by writing 1 as the denominator.

2. Setting Up Proportions

A proportion is an equation that shows two ratios equal to each other.

> *Example 1:* Tammy read 150 pages in 3 days. Write a proportion that shows how to find the number of pages she will read in 5 days.
>
>> **Step 1.** Write the ratio that you know:
>>
>> Write this ratio as pages to days: $\dfrac{150}{3}$
>>
>> Read this ratio as "150 is to 3".
>
>> **Step 2.** Write the unknown ratio by using a letter for the
>>
> unknown number:
>
>> Write this ratio as pages to days, with n standing for the unknown
>>
>> number of days: $\dfrac{n}{5}$
>>
>> Read this ratio as "n is to 5."
>
>> **Step 3.** Write a proportion with the first ratio equal to the second ratio.
>>
>> $\dfrac{150}{3} = \dfrac{n}{5}$
>
> Make sure you set up both ratios the same way. In Example 1, both ratios were set up as pages to days.

> *Example 2:* Popcorn sells for 3 packages for $4 at the supermarket. Write a proportion that shows how much a dozen packages cost.
>
>> Write a ratio using 3 packages for $4: $\dfrac{3}{4}$
>>
>> Change "a dozen packages" to 12 packages.
>>
>> Write the unknown ratio as 12 packages to n: $\dfrac{12}{n}$
>>
>> Write a proportion for these two ratios:
>>
>> $\dfrac{3}{4} = \dfrac{12}{n}$
>
> (In this example, both ratios were set up as packages to cost.)

PRACTICE

Write a ratio for each of these. Reduce the ratios to lowest terms.

1. 10 games won, 4 games lost _____

2. 50 minutes working, 10 minutes resting _____

3. 400 calories for breakfast, 800 calories for dinner _____

4. 1000 students, 50 teachers _____

5. 27 votes for, 18 votes against _____

Choose the correct answers for Questions 6-14.

6. What is the ratio of $\frac{40}{50}$ expressed in lowest terms?

   A. $\frac{8}{10}$

   B. $\frac{10}{8}$

   C. $\frac{4}{5}$

   D. $\frac{5}{4}$

   E. $\frac{4}{9}$

7. Find this ratio: area of grid shaded to area of grid NOT shaded.

   (***Hint***: Remember, a symbol like 1:4 is the same as $\frac{1}{4}$.)

   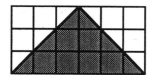

   A. 1:4

   B. 1:3

   C. 1:2

   D. 2:3

   E. 3:4

8. Hamburgers are on special at Steve's Luncheonette. You can buy 2 burgers for $3. Which proportion shows how to find the cost of 10 hamburgers?

   A. $\frac{2}{3} = \frac{n}{10}$

   B. $\frac{2}{3} = \frac{10}{n}$

   C. $\frac{2}{10} = \frac{n}{3}$

   D. $\frac{2}{n} = \frac{10}{3}$

   E. $\frac{3}{2} = \frac{10}{n}$

9. Donna makes $57 every 3 hours giving advice about computers. Which proportion shows how to find how much money she makes in 14 hours?

   A. $\frac{57}{3} = \frac{14}{x}$

   B. $\frac{3}{57} = \frac{x}{14}$

   C. $\frac{57}{3} = \frac{x}{14}$

   D. $\frac{x}{3} = \frac{14}{57}$

   E. $\frac{14}{x} = \frac{57}{3}$

10. A map scale reads 2 cm = 7 km. On the map it is 8 cm from a house to a lake. Which proportion shows how to find the distance from house to lake?

    A. $\frac{8}{2} = \frac{7}{x}$

    B. $\frac{8}{7} = \frac{2}{x}$

    C. $\frac{2}{x} = \frac{7}{8}$

    D. $\frac{2}{8} = \frac{x}{7}$

    E. $\frac{2}{7} = \frac{8}{x}$

11. Jill's car can travel 34 miles on a gallon of gasoline. Which proportion shows how to find how far it should be able to travel on 7 gallons of gasoline?

    A. $\frac{34}{1} = \frac{7}{x}$

    B. $\frac{7}{34} = \frac{x}{1}$

    C. $\frac{7}{1} = \frac{34}{x}$

    D. $\frac{x}{1} = \frac{34}{7}$

    E. $\frac{34}{1} = \frac{x}{7}$

-16-

12. In a group of 50 children, 3 out of 5 have visited the Space Museum. Which proportion shows how to find the number of children who have visited the Space Museum?

    A. $\dfrac{3}{5} = \dfrac{50}{n}$

    B. $\dfrac{3}{50} = \dfrac{5}{n}$

    C. $\dfrac{3}{n} = \dfrac{50}{5}$

    D. $\dfrac{3}{5} = \dfrac{n}{50}$

    E. $\dfrac{n}{3} = \dfrac{5}{50}$

13. A group of students took a vote for their favorite subject. Five students chose art, 3 students chose history, and 2 chose science. Which fraction represents the ratio of students in the class who chose science?

    A. $\dfrac{1}{2}$

    B. $\dfrac{2}{5}$

    C. $\dfrac{1}{3}$

    D. $\dfrac{3}{10}$

    E. $\dfrac{1}{5}$

14. Rename the following ratio as a fraction in lowest terms.

    35:42

    A. $\dfrac{5}{6}$

    B. $\dfrac{6}{5}$

    C. $\dfrac{5}{7}$

    D. $\dfrac{7}{5}$

    E. $\dfrac{35}{42}$

LESSON 7 RATIOS AND PERCENTAGES: Solving Proportions

Example 1: Tammy reads 150 pages in 3 days. How many can she read in 5 days?

Step 1. Set up the proportion for this problem.

We already set up the proportion for this problem—see Lesson 6, p. 15:

$$\frac{150}{3} = \frac{n}{5}$$

Step 2. Find the two **numbers** diagonally opposite each other:

$$\frac{150}{3} \searrow \frac{n}{5}$$

The numbers diagonally opposite each other are 150 and 5.

Step 3. Multiply the two numbers diagonally opposite each other:

$$150 \times 5 = 750$$

Step 4. Divide by the remaining number:

$$750 \div 3 = 250$$

Tammy read 250 pages in 5 days.

Example 2: If a car can travel 42 miles on 1 gallon of gasoline, how far should it be able to travel on 5 gallons of gasoline?

Set up the proportion for this problem:

$$\frac{42}{1} = \frac{n}{5}$$

Multiply the numbers on the diagonal:

$$42 \times 5 = 210$$

Divide by 1: $210 \div 1 = 210$

The car can travel 210 miles on 5 gallons of gasoline.

PRACTICE

Solve these proportions.

1. $\dfrac{x}{30} = \dfrac{4}{10}$ _____

2. $\dfrac{20}{n} = \dfrac{5}{6}$ _____

3. $\dfrac{3}{1} = \dfrac{90}{q}$ _____

4. $\dfrac{3}{4} = \dfrac{30}{t}$ _____

5. $\dfrac{20}{1} = \dfrac{100}{y}$ _____

Choose the correct answers for Questions 6-11.

6. The scale on a map is 2 cm = 50 km. On the map, it is 7 cm from Jacksonville to Centerville. How far is it from Jacksonville to Centerville?
    A. 75 km
    B. 100 km
    C. 125 km
    D. 150 km
    E. 175 km

7. Tim's baseball team wins 7 of every 10 games it plays. If the team played 40 games, how many games did it win?
    A. 14
    B. 21
    C. 28
    D. 32
    E. 35

8. Pencils sell 4 for 37 cents. How much would one dozen cost?
    A. $4.07
    B. $1.48
    C. $1.11
    D. $1.10
    E. $1.00

9. Michael's car can travel 50 kilometers on a gallon of gasoline. How far should it be able to travel on 7 gallons of gasoline?
    A. 200 kilometers
    B. 250 kilometers
    C. 300 kilometers
    D. 350 kilometers
    E. 400 kilometers

10. In a group of 50 children, 1 out of 5 visited the space museum. How many children visited the space museum?
    A. 5
    B. 10
    C. 15
    D. 25
    E. 40

11. Suzanne drove 100 miles in 3 hours. How long will it take her to drive 400 miles?
    A. 16 hours
    B. 12 hours
    C. 10 hours
    D. 8 hours
    E. 6 hours

LESSON 8   RATIOS AND PERCENTAGES: Changing Fractions to Percents

Percent means "compared to 100." So percents are actually fractions with invisible denominators of 100.

1. Fractions with Denominators of 100

Example 1: Write $\frac{23}{100}$ as a percent.

Step 1. Since the denominator of $\frac{23}{100}$ is 100, the percent is the same as the numerator:

$$\frac{23}{100} = 23\%$$

Example 2: Write $\frac{7}{100}$ as a percent

$$\frac{7}{100} = 7\%$$

2. Fractions Whose Denominators Divide 100

Example 1: Write $\frac{4}{5}$ as a percent.

Step 1. Divide 100 by the denominator:

$100 \div 5 = 20$

Step 2. Multiply the numerator by the answer to Step 1:

$4 \times 20 = 80$

Step 3. Write this fraction:

$$\frac{\text{answer to Step 2}}{100} = \frac{80}{100}$$

$\frac{4}{5}$ is equivalent to $\frac{80}{100}$

Step 4. Use the numerator of the new fraction to write the percent:

$$\frac{80}{100} = 80\%$$

So $\frac{4}{5} = 80\%$

Example 2: Write $\frac{3}{4}$ as a percent.

Divide 100 by 4: $100 \div 4 = 25$

Multiply 3 by 25: $3 \times 25 = 75$

Write the fraction: $\frac{75}{100}$

Write the percent: 75%

3. Using a Table

It is useful to remember the percents that are equivalent to some common fractions.

The following table shows common fractions with their equivalent percents. It is a good idea to memorize the conversions from fractions to percents and from percents to fractions.

FRACTION-PERCENT EQUIVALENTS	
Fraction	**Percents**
$\frac{1}{10}$	= 10%
$\frac{1}{5}$	= 20%
$\frac{1}{4}$	= 25%
$\frac{3}{10}$	= 30%
$\frac{1}{3}$	= 33 1/3%
$\frac{2}{5}$	= 40%
$\frac{1}{2}$	= 50%
$\frac{3}{5}$	= 60%
$\frac{2}{3}$	= 66 2/3%
$\frac{7}{10}$	= 70%
$\frac{3}{4}$	= 75%
$\frac{4}{5}$	= 80%
$\frac{9}{10}$	= 90%

Example 1: What percent of the figure is shaded?

Step 1. Find the fraction of the square that is shaded:

$\frac{1}{4}$ of the square is shaded.

Step 2. Convert the fraction to a percent by using the table:

$\frac{1}{4} = 25\%$

PRACTICE

Write the percent for each of these fractions.

1. $\frac{35}{100}$ _____

2. $\frac{7}{100}$ _____

3. $\frac{57}{100}$ _____

4. $\frac{1}{4}$ _____

5. $\frac{3}{5}$ _____

6. $\frac{1}{2}$ _____

Choose the correct answer for each of these.

7. Write $\frac{1}{5}$ as a percent.

   A. 10%

   B. 15%

   C. 20%

   D. 25%

   E. 30%

8. How is $\frac{3}{100}$ expressed as a percent?

   A. 300%

   B. 30%

   C. 33%

   D. 3%

   E. 0.3%

9. 30% equals

    A. $\frac{3}{1}$

    B. $\frac{30}{50}$

    C. $\frac{3}{100}$

    D. $\frac{30}{100}$

    E. $\frac{300}{100}$

10. Which is equal to $\frac{1}{4}$?

    A. 14%

    B. 20%

    C. 25%

    D. 35%

    E. 50%

11. Write $\frac{4}{5}$ as a percent.

    A. 20%

    B. 25%

    C. 45%

    D. 60%

    E. 80%

12. Bert spelled 80 of his 100 words correctly. What percent of his words did he spell correctly?

    A. 8%

    B. 10%

    C. 20%

    D. 80%

    E. 120%

13. What percent of the circle is shaded?

(**_Hint:_** Find the fraction of the circle shaded, then use the table in Section 3, p. 21, above.)

    A. $\frac{2}{5}$%

    B. 20%

    C. 40%

    D. 60%

    E. 120%

LESSON 9   RATIOS AND PERCENTAGES:
Changing Percents to Fractions and Decimals

1. Changing Percents to Fractions

Example 1: Write 35% as a fraction in lowest terms.

Step 1. Write the percent as a fraction with a denominator of 100:

35% is the same as $\frac{35}{100}$.

Step 2. Reduce the fraction to lowest terms:

$\frac{35}{100} = \frac{7}{20}$

35% is the same as $\frac{7}{20}$.

Example 2: Write 70% as a fraction in lowest terms.

Write 70% as a fraction with a denominator of 100:

$70\% = \frac{70}{100}$.

Reduce $\frac{70}{100}$ to lowest terms: $\frac{70}{100} = \frac{7}{10}$

Example 3: Write 9% as a fraction in lowest terms.

Write 9% as $\frac{9}{100}$

$\frac{9}{100}$ cannot be reduced.

2. Changing Percents to Decimals

Example 1: Write 48% as a decimal number.

Step 1. Drop the % sign:

35% becomes 35.

Step 2. Move the decimal point **two places** to the left:

.35x

35% is the same as 0.35.

Example 2: Write 60% as a decimal.

Drop the % sign: 60% becomes 60.

Move the decimal point two places to the left: .60x

0.60 is equivalent to 60%

Example 3: Write 3% as a decimal.

Drop the % sign: 3% becomes 3.

Move the decimal point 2 places to the left.

Add a 0 to the hundredths place: .03.

3% = 0.03

PRACTICE

Write the fraction in lowest terms for each percent.

1. 23% = _____

2. 45% = _____

3. 80% = _____

4. 5% = _____

Write the decimal for each percent.

5. 56% = _____

6. 91% = _____

7. 3% = _____

8. 8% = _____

Choose the correct answer for Questions 9-12.

9. Write 2% as a fraction in lowest terms.

A. $\frac{2}{100}$

B. $\frac{2}{50}$

C. $\frac{1}{50}$

D. $\frac{1}{100}$

E. $\frac{2}{10}$

11. Which of these is true?

A. $25\% = \frac{13}{20}$

B. $35\% = \frac{13}{20}$

C. $45\% = \frac{13}{20}$

D. $55\% = \frac{13}{20}$

E. $65\% = \frac{13}{20}$

10. Which renames 4% as a decimal?

A. 0.0004

B. 0.004

C. 0.04

D. 0.4

E. 4

12. Which decimal is equivalent to 92%?

A. 9.2

B. 0.92

C. 0.092

D. 0.0092

E. 0.00092

LESSON 10   RATIOS AND PERCENTAGES: Finding the Percent of a Total

1. Converting to a Fraction

Example 1: What is 25% of 200?

    Step 1. Change the percent to a fraction.

$$25\% = \frac{25}{100}$$

    Reduce 25/100 to lowest terms: $\frac{25}{100} = \frac{1}{4}$

    Step 2. Multiply by the fraction:

$$\frac{1}{4} \times 200 = \frac{1}{4} \times \frac{200}{1} = 50$$

    So 25% of 200 is 50.

Example 2: Fifty percent of the 120 students at the science museum were girls. How many girls were at the science museum?

    Change 50% to a fraction:

$$50\% = \frac{50}{100} = \frac{1}{2}$$

    Multiply: $\frac{1}{2} \times 120 = \frac{1}{2} \times \frac{120}{1} = 60$

60 girls were at the science museum.

2. Using a Table

The following table shows common percents with their equivalent fractions. This table is like the one in Lesson 8, except the two columns are reversed. Memorize it!

PERCENT –FRACTION EQUIVALENTS

%	Fraction	%	Fraction
10%	$\frac{1}{10}$	60%	$\frac{3}{5}$
20%	$\frac{1}{5}$	$66\frac{2}{3}\%$	$\frac{2}{3}$
25%	$\frac{1}{4}$	70%	$\frac{7}{10}$
30%	$\frac{3}{10}$	75%	$\frac{3}{4}$
$33\frac{1}{3}\%$	$\frac{1}{3}$	80%	$\frac{4}{5}$
40%	$\frac{2}{5}$	90%	$\frac{9}{10}$
50%	$\frac{1}{2}$		

Example 1: In a science museum, 40% of the computer games are about animals. If there are 80 computer games in the museum, how many are about animals?

Use the table to find the fraction equivalent to 40%.

$40\% = \frac{2}{5}$.

Multiply: $\frac{2}{5} \times 80 = \frac{2}{5} \times \frac{80}{1} = 32$

There are 32 computer games about animals.

PRACTICE

Write the fraction for each percent.

1. 23% = _____

2. 70% = _____

3. 40% = _____

4. 75% = _____

5. $66\frac{2}{3}\%$ = _____

6. 8%

Compute the percent.

7. What is 50% of 500?   _____

8. What is 25% of 80?   _____

9. What is 10% of 450?   _____

10. What is 60% of 80?   _____

11. What is 5% of 2000?   _____

12. What is 40% of 30?   _____

Choose the correct answer.

13. Ozzie made $300 last week. Thirty percent was from mowing lawns. How much did he make mowing lawns?

    A. $30

    B. $40

    C. $50

    D. $60

    E. $90

14. Peggy lost 50% of her 30-page report. How many pages did she lose?

    A. 5

    B. 10

    C. 15

    D. 20

    E. 25

15. Bob made 80% of his foul shots. If he tried 50 foul shots, how many did he make?

    A. 20

    B. 30

    C. 40

    D. 50

    E. 60

16 Jackie spent $150 over the last week. According to the graph, how much did she spend on clothing?

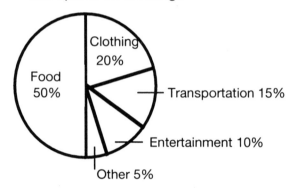

    A. $100

    B. $75

    C. $50

    D. $30

    E. $15

LESSON 11 MEASUREMENT: Estimating Length

Measurement questions sometimes test whether you understand the difference among units of measurement. You have to know that a pencil is about 6 centimeters long, not 6 meters long or 6 millimeters long.

To help you review, here are descriptions of several common units.

Length

millimeter (mm)—a small length; a dime is about a millimeter thick.

centimeter (cm)—about half an inch; the width of a fingernail; about this long: _____

meter (m)—little more than a yard

inch (in.)—the width of the joint on your thumb; about this long: _____

foot (ft)—This page is almost a foot long.

yard (yd)—the length you get when you spread your arms like wings

Example 1: Is a paper clip closer to 3 mm long or 3 cm long?

    Step 1. Think of a paper clip—

        You have to choose the length that fits best.

    Step 2. Think how long a millimeter is—see the table above.

        A millimeter is about the width of a dime.

    Step 3. Think how long a centimeter is—see the table above.

        A centimeter is about this long _____

    Step 4. Choose the length that is closest to the paper clip: 3 mm or 3 cm

        3 mm is too small. 3 cm seems just right.

The paper clip is about 3 cm long.

Example 2: Which of these is the best estimate for the length of an automobile?

    A. 4 mm

    B. 4 cm

    C. 4 m

    D. 4 in.

    E. 4 ft

Look at the answer choices. Each one uses a different unit of length.

Answer Choice A uses millimeters. A millimeter is about the thickness of a dime. It is much too small.

Answer Choice B uses centimeters. A centimeter is about the width of one of your fingernails. It is also much too small.

Answer Choice C uses meters. A meter is a little longer than a yard. It is a good unit to measure the length of a car. A car is about 4 meters long, so this choice looks as if it is correct. But we should check the other two choices anyway.

Answer Choice D uses inches. An inch is about the width of the joint on your thumb. It is too small to measure cars.

Answer Choice E uses feet. A foot is a little less than the length of this page. It could be used as a unit to measure the length of a car, but 4 feet is too small.

PRACTICE

1. Which line segment is approximately 2 inches long?
   A. ___
   B. _____
   C. _____
   D. _____
   E. _____

2. Which line is about 4 centimeters long?
   A. _____
   B. _____
   C. _____
   D. ___
   E. _

3. Which line is 10 millimeters long?
   A. _
   B. _____
   C. _____
   D. _____
   E. _____

4. What would be the best estimate of the length of a toothpick?
   A. 7 mm
   B. 7 cm
   C. 7 m
   D. 7 ft
   E. 7 yd

5. What unit of length would you use to measure the thickness of an aspirin?

    A. mm
    B. cm
    C. m
    D. in.
    E. ft

6. What unit of length would you use to measure the height of a house?

    A. mm
    B. cm
    C. m
    D. in.
    E. g

7. What unit of length would you use to measure the length of a football field?

    A. mm
    B. cm
    C. oz
    D. in.
    E. yd

8. Which of these is the best estimate for the length of a teacher's desk?

    A. 1 foot
    B. 2 feet
    C. 4 feet
    D. 8 feet
    E. 20 inches

9. Which of these is the best estimate for the length of a new swimming pool in a school?

    A. 50 m
    B. 50 cm
    C. 50 lb
    D. 50 in.
    E. 50 ft

10. Which of these would you use to measure the length of a leg of an ant?

    A. mm
    B. cm
    C. m
    D. in.
    E. ft

LESSON 12 MEASUREMENT: Making Change

Example 1: Fran spent $5.95 for juice and $2.19 for bread at the supermarket. How much change did she get from $10?

You can solve this problem in two steps.

      Step 1. Add the two amounts Fran spent.

          Add: $5.95 + 2.19 = $8.14

      Step 2. Subtract to find the change.

          Subtract: $10.00 - 8.14 = $1.86

      Fran got $1.86 change from $10.

Example 2: Jimmy bought two CDs for $15.98 each. The total sales tax for this purchase was $1.60. How much change did Jimmy get from $40?

      Add the amounts of the two purchases:

          $15.95 + 15.95 = $31.90

      Add the sales tax to the total of the purchases:

          $31.90 + 1.60 = $33.50

      Subtract the total from $40: $40 - 33.50 = $6.50

      Jimmy got $6.50 in change.

PRACTICE

Find the change for each of these purchases:

	Cost of Purchase	Paid With	Change
1.	$14.56	$20	_____
2.	$7.45	$10	_____
3.	$22.50	$25	_____
4.	$38.40	$40	_____
5.	$7.24	$10	_____

Choose the correct answer for Questions 6-11.

6. Doug bought two tickets to the baseball game at $7.45 each. How much change did he get from $20?
   A. $4.10
   B. $4.50
   C. $4.90
   D. $5.10
   E. $5.20

7. You purchased two pizzas for $10.95 each at your favorite restaurant. The sales tax was $1.10. How much change did you get from $25?
   A. $4.90
   B. $4.10
   C. $3.10
   D. $2.10
   E. $2.00

8. Bill paid $12.50 for a book and $2.95 for a magazine. How much change did he get from $20?
   A. $4.55
   B. $4.45
   C. $4.35
   D. $4.25
   E. $4.15

9. Nancy paid $3.50 for a hamburger and $1.25 for a large soda. If the tax for her meal was $.24, how much change did she get from $10?
   A. $3.99
   B. $4.01
   C. $4.75
   D. $4.99
   E. $5.01

10. Margo bought a hockey stick for $22 and a helmet for $28.50. How much change did she get from 60 dollars?
   A. $19.50
   B. $19
   C. $15.50
   D. $9.50
   E. $9

11. Esther works in a hardware store where a customer gives her $25 to pay for a bill that comes to $24.15. What is the correct change she should give the customer using the fewest coins possible?
   A. 3 quarters
   B. 3 quarters, 2 nickels
   C. 2 quarters, 4 dimes
   D. 3 quarters, 1 dime
   E. 3 quarters, 1 dime, 1 nickel

LESSON 13   MEASUREMENT: Elapsed Time

Example 1: If Kathy works from 7:45 A.M. until 11:30 A.M., how long does she work?

Step 1. Compute the number of **full hours** that elapsed.

Compute the number of hours from 7:45 A.M. until 10:45 A.M. That is 3 hours from 7:45 until 10:45.

Step 2 Compute the number of **minutes** from 10:45 A.M. to 11:30 A.M.

It is 45 minutes from 10:45 until 11:30.

Step 3 Combine the results of Steps 1 and 2:

Number of hours: 3

Number of minutes: 45

Total time elapsed: 3 hours 45 minutes

Example 2: Burt started mowing his lawn at 3:15 P.M. and finished $2\frac{1}{2}$ hours later. When did he finish?

Break up 2 1/2 hours into 2 hours and 1/2 hour.

Add 2 hours to 3:15: that makes the time 5:15.

Change 1/2 hour to 30 minutes.

Add 30 minutes to 5:15: that make the time 5:45.

Burt finished at 5:45 P.M.

PRACTICE

Compute the amount of time elapsed from the starting time to the finishing time.

	Starting Time	Finishing Time	Time Elapsed
1.	2:30 P.M.	7:30 P.M.	_____
2.	4:15 A.M.	7:00 A.M.	_____
3.	11:30 A.M.	2:30 P.M.	_____
4.	4:05 A.M.	9:00 A.M.	_____
5.	6:25 P.M.	11:10 P.M.	_____
6.	8:35 A.M.	1:10 P.M.	_____

Compute the finishing time from the starting time and the amount of time elapsed.

	Starting Time	Time Elapsed	Finishing Time
7.	4:45 P.M.	4 hours	_____
8.	3:20 A.M.	12 hours	_____
9.	8:10 A.M.	3 hours 20 minutes	_____
10.	4:15 P.M.	2 hours 50 minutes	_____

Choose the correct answer for Questions 11-12.

11. Marge spent 4 hours 15 minutes watching movies. If she started at 6:30 P.M., at what time did she finish?

    A. 9:45 P.M.

    B. 10:00 P.M.

    C. 10:15 P.M.

    D. 10:30 P.M.

    E. 10:45 P.M.

12. Mike came to the barbecue at 6:45 P.M. and left at 10:10 P.M. How long did he stay?

    A. 3 hours

    B. 3 hours 5 minutes

    C. 3 hours 15 minutes

    D. 3 hours 25 minutes

    E. 3 hours 35 minutes

LESSON 14 ALGEBRA:
Finding the Missing Symbol to Complete a Sentence

Example 1: What number completes this sentence?

$$\Box \div 3 = 2 \times 6$$

Step 1. Notice that you can find the answer to only one side of the equation. The other side has an unknown number.

You can find the answer to the right-hand side (2 x 6).

The left-hand side has the unknown number.

Step 2. Compute the value of the right-hand side.

The right hand side equals 12.

Step 3. Read the equation by replacing $\Box$ with the words "what number?"

$$\Box \div 3 = 12$$

"What number divided by 3 equals 12?"

Step 4. Find the missing number.

36 divided by 3 equals 12.

The missing number is 36.

All IGAP test questions ask that you choose the correct answer. When you choose a missing symbol for a sentence, keep an eye on the answer choices as you work out the problem.

Example 2: Which symbol in the box makes this a true sentence?

$$1\frac{2}{3} \ \Box \ \frac{4}{2}$$

Here are the choices:

A. =

B. <

C. >

D. -

E. +

To find out which answer to choose, change the mixed number into an improper fraction:

$$1\frac{2}{3} = \frac{5}{3}$$

Replace $1\frac{2}{3}$ with $\frac{5}{3}$ in the sentence:

$$\frac{5}{3} \ \square \ \frac{4}{2}$$

Since $\frac{5}{3}$ is **greater than** $\frac{4}{3}$, the symbol that makes the sentence true is >. The answer is C.

Example 3: Which symbol in the box makes this a true sentence?

$$\frac{1}{5} \ \square \ 40\%$$

Here are the choices:

     A. ÷

     B. x

     C. =

     D. <

     E. >

To find which answer works, change 40% to a fraction. Then reduce the fraction to lowest terms.

$$40\% = \frac{40}{100} = \frac{2}{5}$$

Replace 40% with $\frac{2}{5}$:

$$\frac{1}{5} \ \square \ \frac{2}{5}$$

Since 1/5 is less than 2/5, the symbol that makes the sentence true is <. The answer is D.

PRACTICE

What number makes each sentence true?

1. $\square$ x 4 = 2 x 8   Missing number: _____

2. 27 - 3 = $\square$ ÷ 2   Missing number: _____

3. 23 + $\square$ = 2 x 18   Missing number: _____

Which symbol in the box makes each sentence true? Choose the correct answer.

4. $\frac{4}{5}$ ☐ 80%

    A. +

    B. -

    C. =

    D. <

    E. >

5. 40% ☐ $\frac{1}{2}$

    A. x

    B. ÷

    C. =

    D. <

    E. >

6. $1\frac{3}{5}$ ☐ $\frac{9}{5}$

    A. x

    B. ÷

    C. =

    D. <

    E. >

7. $3\frac{1}{6}$ ☐ $\frac{19}{6}$

    A. =

    B. ÷

    C. <

    D. >

    E. +

8. $2\frac{1}{4}$ ☐ $\frac{9}{4}$

    A. -

    B. x

    C. <

    D. >

    E. =

9. 50% ☐ $\frac{3}{5}$

    A. =

    B. <

    C. >

    D. -

    E. x

10. $\frac{9}{10}$ ☐ 90%

    A. =

    B. <

    C. >

    D. -

    E. x

11. 3.55 - 1.3 ☐ 2.25

    A. =

    B. <

    C. >

    D. -

    E. x

12. If n < 12, then n could equal

    A. 11

    B. 12

    C. 13

    D. 14

    E. 15

LESSON 15 ALGEBRA:
Translating Word Problems into Equations

You need to know how to translate phrases into math sentences.

Here is a table of common phrases and how they translate into mathematical symbols.

Phrases Meaning Addition

3 plus 4	3 + 4
add 5 and z	5 + z
increase 12 by 8	12 + 8 (or 8 + 12)
the sum of 10 and x	10 + x

Phrases Meaning Subtraction (Be careful. The order of the numbers is important.)

z minus 5	z - 5
subtract 3 from k	k - 3 (not 3 - k)
decrease 20 by 8	20 - 8 (not 8 - 20)
t less 5	t - 5
the difference of c from 18	18 - c (not c - 18)
5 less t	5 - t

Phrases Meaning Multiplication

7 times 9	7 x 9 or 7 · 9
7 times q	7q
multiply r and s	rs
the product of j and k	jk
the product of 4 and x	4x

Phrases Meaning Division

divide m by 13	$\dfrac{m}{13}$
x divided by 17	$\dfrac{x}{17}$
the quotient of z divided by 8	$\dfrac{z}{8}$
r over 92	$\dfrac{r}{92}$

Example 1: Write a number sentence that describes this sentence:

The product of a number and 5 equals the sum of 30 and 5.

Step 1. Find the key words that help translate the words into symbols.

The key words are **_product_**, **_equals_**, and **_sum_**.

Step 2. Determine if the sentence is an equation or an inequality.

Equals means the sentence will be an equation.

Less than or **_more than_** means that the sentence will be an inequality.

Step 3. Translate the key words (see the table on the previous page) one at a time to write an equation.

The product of a number and 5: **_5n_**

The sum of 30 and 5: **_30 + 5 = 35_**

Equation: 5n = 35

Example 2: Phil bought 3 basketballs for $15.75 each. He also bought a soccer ball for $23. Write an equation that can be used to find the total cost of all three items.

Translate the cost of the 3 basketballs: 3 x $15.25

The problem asks for the total cost, so the equation will <u>add</u> the costs together:

Total cost (T) = cost of basketballs + cost of soccer ball

T = 3 x $15.25 + $23

PRACTICE

Write an equation for each of these sentences. Use the letter N as the variable.

1. The sum of 4 and another number equals 28. _____

2. A number decreased by 20 equals 50. _____

3. The quotient of a number divided by 6 equals 48. _____

4. The product of 7 and a number is equal to 97. _____

5. The difference of a number from 3 is equal to 22. _____

6. Decrease a number by 20, then add 4; the result equals 100. _____

7. Multiplying a number times 5 equals the sum of 100 and 35. _____

8. A number less 30 equals the product of 8 and 9. _____

Choose the equation that should be used for each.

9. A baby sitter charges $10 for the first hour and $6 for each hour afterwards. Which equation shows how much she charges for 5 hours of babysitting?

    A. C = 10 x 6 + 4
    B. C = 10 + 4 x 6
    C. C = 10 x 6 + 4
    D. C = 10 + 4 x 10
    E. C = 6 + 4 x 10

10. Joanna receives $12 per hour when she works at the coffee shop. Last week she earned $372. Which equation shows how many hours she worked?

    A. 372 x 12 = N
    B. 372 - 12 = N
    C. 372 + 12 = N
    D. 372 ÷ 12 = N
    E. 372 + 372 = N

11. Which equation best describes the sentence: The product of 9 and 7 equals the sum of a number and 6.

    A. 9 + 7 = 6N
    B. 9 + 7 = N + 6
    C. 9 x 7 = 6N
    D. 9 x 7 = N - 6
    E. 9 x 7 = N + 6

12. Lisa weighed 112 pounds two months ago. Then she lost 4 pounds and gained 2 pounds. Which one of these number sentences could be used to solve this problem?

    A. (112 - 4) + 2 = □
    B. 112 - (4 + 2) = □
    C. - 4 + 2 = 112 + □
    D. (112 + 2) + 4 = □
    E. (112 - 4) - 2 = □

13. Lynne has 2 quarters and Kathy has 5 dimes. Which sentence shows the amount of money Lynne and Kathy have together?

    A. 2 + 5 = □
    B. 2 + 25 + 5 + 10 = □
    C. 2 x 10 + 5 x 25 = □
    D. 2 x 25 + 5 x 10 = □
    E. 7 x (25 + 10) = □

LESSON 16   ALGEBRA:
Solving Equations

Example 1: What is the value of T if

$$170 = T + 65 \ ?$$

To solve an equation, get the variable by itself.

To do that, subtract 65 from both sides:

$$170 - \mathbf{65} = T + 65 - \mathbf{65}$$

$$115 = T \ or$$

$$T = 115$$

Example 2: Solve for Q:

$$3 + (5 + 8) = (8 + 2) + Q$$

Remove the parentheses:

$$3 + 5 + 8 = 8 + 2 + Q$$

Add the numbers on each side of the equation:

$$16 = 10 + Q$$

Subtract 10 from both sides:

$$16 - \mathbf{10} = 10 + Q - \mathbf{10}$$

$$6 = Q \ or$$

$$Q = 6$$

Example 3: If $7 \times (8 + 9) = m$,

$$m = ?$$

Add inside the parentheses: $8 + 9 = 17$

Multiply: $7 \times 17 = 119$

$$m = 119$$

Another way to "see" this equation is as an example of the distributive property:

$$7 \times (8 + 9) \ = \ 7 \times 8 + 7 \times 9 \ = \ 56 + 63 \ = \ 119$$

PRACTICE

Solve each equation for the variable N:

1. 3 + (4 + 7) = (3 + 4) + N   N = __10__

(**Hint**: This is an example of the associative property for addition.)

2. (9 + 8) - 2 = 3N   N = __3__

3. N ÷ 6 = 22   N = __132__

4. 5 x N = 35   N = __7__

5. 70 - N = 61   N = __9__

Choose the correct answer for each of the following questions.

6. Find the value of □ if

   □ ÷ 3 = 6 x 2

   A. 36
   B. 30
   C. 24
   D. 18
   E. 12

7. Which of these equations has the

   same solution as 24 - 18 = □ ?

   A.
   □ + 18 = 12
   B. 18 + □ = 24
   C. 6 + □ = 24
   D. 18 - □ = 24
   E. □ - 12 = 6

8. What is the value of N if

   100 = N + 76 ?

   A. 23
   B. 24
   C. 33
   D. 34

E. 54

9. Find the value of □ if

   □ ÷ 2 = 16 x 3

   A. 36
   B. 48
   C. 72
   D. 96
   E. 144

10. Solve for N.

   6 x (7 + 9) = N

   A. 16
   B. 96
   C. 100
   D. 116
   E. 120

-43-

LESSON 17 ALGEBRA:
Locating and Identifying Points on a Grid

What is an **ordered pair** of numbers? It is a set of two numbers such as (5,7).

* 5 is the first number of the ordered pair, and

* 7 is the second number.

* The first number is called the **x-number**,

* The second number is called the **y-number**.

Each ordered pair can be represented by a point on a grid.

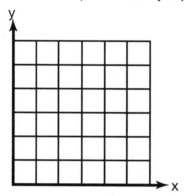

Example 1: Locate a point on the grid for this pair of numbers: (3, 2)

    Step 1. Start by locating the **origin**.

        The origin is the place where the two axes meet.

    Step 2. Move along the x-axis the same distance (number of lines) as the x-number.

        Move along the x-axis 3 units to the **right** of the origin.

    Step 3. Move in the direction of the y-axis the same distance as the y-number.

        Move **up** 2 units.

Step 4. Place a dot at this point.

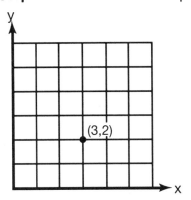

Example 2: Which point indicates the ordered pair (2,4)?

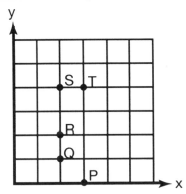

Start at the origin. Move along the x-axis for 2 units.

Then move up 4 units.

You have located the point for (2,4)—it is S.

PRACTICE

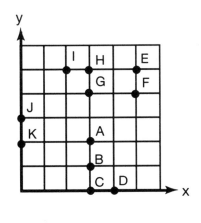

Six of the points on the grid at the left match the ordered pairs below. Write the letter of the point that matches each ordered pair

1. (3,1) _____

2. (0,3) _____

3. (3,4) _____

4. (4,0) _____

5. (5,4) _____

6. (2,5) _____

Choose the correct answers to Questions 7-10.

7. Which point indicates the ordered pair (0,4)?

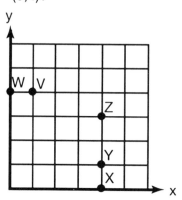

   A. X
   B. Y
   C. Z
   D. W
   E. V

9. Which point shows the ordered pair (4,5)?

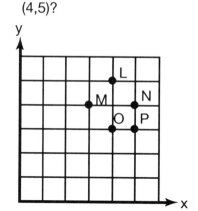

   A. L
   B. M
   C. N
   D. O
   E. P

8. What are the coordinates of point P?

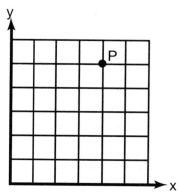

   A. (3,5)
   B. (3,7)
   C. (4,5)
   D, (6,4)
   E. (4,7)

10. What are the coordinates of point Z?

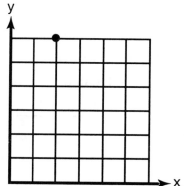

   A. (1,2)
   B. (2,6)
   C. (6,2)
   D. (2,7)
   E. (3,7)

LESSON 18   ALGEBRA: Patterns

Mathematics is full of patterns. There are three ways that you are likely to see patterns.

1. Patterns in a Series of Numbers

Here is a series of numbers:

$$2, 4, 6, 8, 10, \ldots$$

The pattern is the even numbers. The next number in the pattern is 12.

    Example 1: What is the next number that would appear in the following series?

$$1, 2, 4, 7, 11, \_\_\_\_$$

        Step 1. Determine if the numbers get larger or smaller.

           In this set of numbers, the numbers get larger.

        Step 2. Find the differences between the numbers.

           First, find the difference between the 1st and 2nd numbers.

           Then find the difference between the 2nd and 3rd numbers, and so forth.

                Difference between 1st and 2nd numbers: 2 - 1 = 1

                Difference between 2nd and 3rd numbers: 4 - 2 = 2

                Difference between 3rd and 4th numbers: 7 - 4 = 3

                Difference between 4th and 5th numbers: 11 - 7 = 4

        Step 3. Notice the pattern among the differences:

           The differences are 1, 2, 3, 4.

           They increase by 1—that is the pattern.

        Step 4. Find the next number.

           The next number has to be 5 more than the last number:

$$11 + 5 = 16.$$

        The next number is 16.

    Example 2: Find the next number of the series:

$$34, 29, 24, 19, 14, \_\_\_$$

The numbers are decreasing. Find the differences between the numbers:

$$34 - 29 = 5$$

$$29 - 24 = 5$$

$$24 - 19 = 5$$
$$19 - 14 = 5$$

The numbers decrease by 5—that is the pattern.

To find the next number, subtract 5:

$$14 - 5 = 9$$

The next number is 9.

2. Patterns in a Table

Example 1: What is the missing number?

X	Y
4	11
9	16
12	19
15	?
20	27

Step 1. Find the difference between the x-numbers and y-numbers for all pairs of known x-numbers and y-numbers:

$$11 - 4 = 7$$
$$16 - 9 = 7$$
$$19 - 12 = 7$$
$$27 - 20 = 7$$

Step 2. Observe the pattern:

The pattern is: the y-numbers are 7 more than the x-numbers.

Step 3. Use the pattern to find the missing number:

$$15 + 7 = 22$$

The missing number is 22.

3. **Patterns with Geometric Figures**

___***Example 1:***___ What figure comes next?

Step 1. Give each figure a number starting from 1.

From left to right, circle = 1; square = 2; triangle = 3; rectangle = 4.

① ② ③ ④ ① ②

Step 2. Ask yourself: What number comes next?

The next number in the sequence is 3

Step 3. Match this number to its figure:

The number 3 stands for the triangle.

The next figure is the triangle.

PRACTICE

Find the next number for each of these series.

1. 1, 3, 5, 7, 9, ___

2. 2, 5, 8, 11, 14, ___

3. 30, 25, 20, 15, 10, ___

(___**Hint**___: In this series the numbers get smaller.)

4. 2, 4, 8, 16, ___

5. 3, 8, 13, 18, 23, ___

6. 40, 36, 32, 28, 24, ___

Choose the correct answer for Questions 7-10.

7. What is the missing number?

X	Y
2	6
7	11
12	16
18	?
32	36

A. 16
B. 18
C. 20
D. 22
E. 24

8. What is the next number that would appear in the series?

7, 9, 13, 19, 27, ____

A. 29
B. 31
C. 33
D. 35
E. 37

9. What is the next number that would appear in the series?

48, 42, 36, 30, 24, ____

A. 30
B. 22
C. 20
D. 18
E. 16

10. What is the missing number?

X	Y
27	18
22	13
20	11
12	?
10	1

A. 1
B. 2
C. 3
D. 4
E. 5

In Questions 11 and 12, find the next figure in the pattern.

11.

○ ○ □ ▷ ○ ○ □

A. □
B. ▷
C. ▭
D. ○
E. △

12.

□ ○ □ △ □ ○

A. □
B. ▷
C. ▭
D. ○
E. △

LESSON 19 GEOMETRY: Angles

1. Types of Angles

You need to know the four different types of angles.

Right angle—an angle that forms a corner; it measures 90°.

Acute angle—an angle whose measure is less than 90°.

Obtuse angle—an angle whose measure is greater than 90°.

Straight angle—an angle that forms a straight line; it measures 180°.

Example 1: What type of angle is angle B in this diagram?

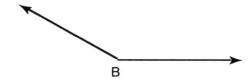

B

This angle is more than 90°, so it is an obtuse angle.

Example 2: Which angle in this figure appears to be a right angle?

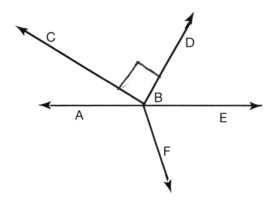

A. ∠ABC

B. ∠CBD

C. ∠DBE

D. ∠ABF

E. ∠EBF

There are many angles that you can find here. Search for one that forms a square corner. It appears to be ∠CBD, even though the corner is rotated.

Example 3: Which sides of ABCD are part of ∠BCD?

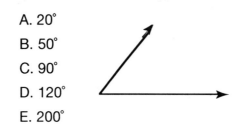

On the figure, use a pencil to draw on ∠BCD.

The sides that make up ∠BCD are $\overline{BC}$ and $\overline{CD}$.

2. **Finding the Measure of an Angle**

Example 1: What is the measure of this angle?

A. 20°

B. 50°

C. 90°

D. 120°

E. 200°

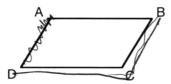

-52-

Step 1. Determine which type of angle this is.

This is an acute angle—less than 90°.

Step 2. Eliminate answers based upon the type of angle.

Since the angle is an acute angle, you can eliminate 90° (this is a right angle) and measures greater than 90° (those are obtuse angles). So you can eliminate answers C, D, and E.

Step 3. Choose the best answer from A and B.

The angle looks about half of a right angle. Half a right angle is 45°.

50° is closer to 45° than 20°.

So the answer is B.

Example 2: In the figure below, what is the measure of ∠APC? Choose the correct answer.

A. 30°
B. 40°
C. 60°
D. 140°
E. 180°

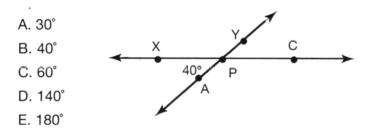

It should be clear from the diagram that ∠APC is an obtuse angle. It is greater than 90°. You can eliminate answers A, B, and C—these are measures of acute angles. Answer E cannot be the answer, since an angle of 180° is a straight angle. By using the process of elimination, the answer is D.

PRACTICE

Identify each of these angles as acute, obtuse, right, or straight.

1. 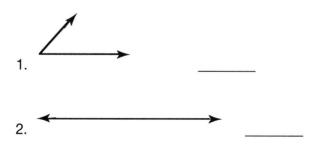 _____

2. _____

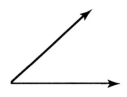

3. _____

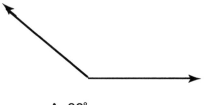

4. _____

For Questions 5-11 choose the correct answer.

5. What is the measure of ∠XYZ in the
   figure below? _____

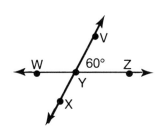

(**Hint**: Remember, ∠WYZ is a straight
angle, equal to 180°.)

    A. 20°
    B. 30°
    C. 40°
    D. 120°
    E. 180°

6. Estimate the measure of this angle.

    A. 40°
    B. 80°
    C. 90°
    D. 120°
    E. 150°

7. Estimate the measure of this angle.

    A. 20°
    B. 60°
    C. 90°
    D. 140°
    E. 180°

8. What is the measure of ∠MOP in the
   figure below?

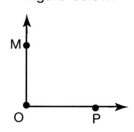

    A. 50°
    B. 60°
    C. 70°
    D. 80°
    E. 90°

9. Each corner of this table top forms a

    A. circle

    B. rectangle

    C. right angle

    D. square

    E. straight angle

10. What is the measure of ∠SOV in the figure below?

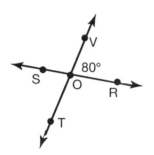

    A. 70°

    B. 80°

    C. 90°

    D. 100°

    E. 170

11. Which sides of XYZW are part of ∠XYZ?

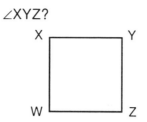

    A. XY and YZ

    B. YZ and ZX

    C. ZW and WX

    D. WX and XY

    E. XY and ZW

LESSON 20   GEOMETRY:
Parallel and Perpendicular Lines

1. Parallel Lines

Lines that are always the same distance apart are called **parallel** lines.

Example 1: Which line is parallel to line q?

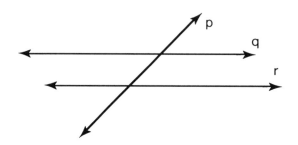

Step 1. Remember that parallel means lines that are always the same distance apart.

Step 2. Look for lines that are the same distance apart.

Line r is always the same distance from line q.

Line r is parallel to line q.

2. Perpendicular Lines

Lines that cross each other at right angles are called **perpendicular** lines.

Example 1: Which line is perpendicular to line a?

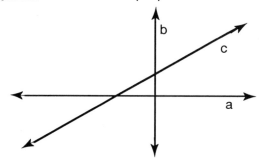

Step 1. Remember what _perpendicular_ means: lines crossing at right angles, and that _right angles_ means square corners.

Step 2. Look for corners—that is where you will find perpendicular lines.

Line b makes a square corner with line a.

Line b is perpendicular to line a.

PRACTICE

Check the correct answer in Questions 1-5.

1. Are the line segments parallel,
   perpendicular, or neither?

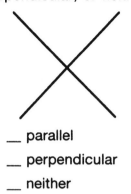

   __ parallel
   __ perpendicular
   __ neither

2. Are the lines parallel, perpendicular, or
   neither?

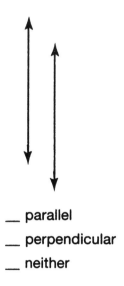

   __ parallel
   __ perpendicular
   __ neither

3. Are the lines parallel, perpendicular, or
   neither?

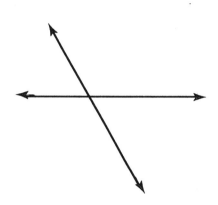

   __ parallel
   __ perpendicular
   __ neither

4. Are lines a and b parallel,
   perpendicular, or neither?

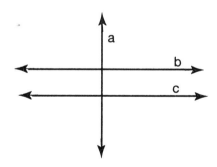

   __ parallel
   __ perpendicular
   __ neither

-57-

5. Are lines x and y parallel, perpendicular, or neither?

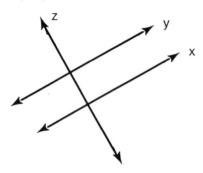

___ parallel

___ perpendicular

___ neither

Choose the correct answer for Questions 6-10.

6. Which of the following statements is correct?

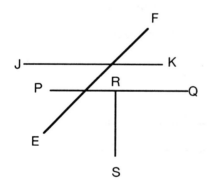

A. $\overline{PQ}$ is parallel to $\overline{RS}$.

B. $\overline{PQ}$ is perpendicular to $\overline{RS}$.

C. $\overline{PQ}$ is perpendicular to $\overline{JK}$.

D. $\overline{EF}$ is parallel to $\overline{RS}$.

E. $\overline{JK}$ is parallel to $\overline{RS}$.

7. Which edge is parallel to edge ZW?

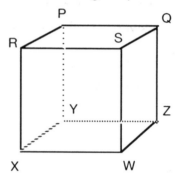

A. $\overline{QR}$

B. $\overline{SW}$

C. $\overline{XY}$

D. $\overline{YZ}$

E. $\overline{XW}$

8. Which segment is perpendicular to $\overline{MN}$?

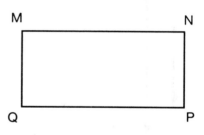

A. $\overline{NP}$

B. $\overline{PQ}$

C. $\overline{QM}$

D. $\overline{MP}$

E. $\overline{NQ}$

9. Which edge is parallel to edge $\overline{PQ}$?

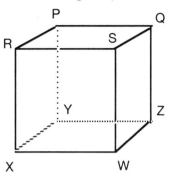

    A. $\overline{QZ}$

    B. $\overline{SW}$

    C. $\overline{YZ}$

    D. $\overline{XY}$

    E. $\overline{ZW}$

10. Which of the following statements is correct?

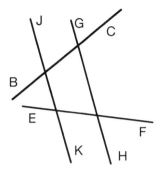

    A. $\overline{BC}$ is parallel to $\overline{EF}$.

    B. $\overline{BC}$ is perpendicular to $\overline{EF}$.

    C. $\overline{BC}$ is perpendicular to $\overline{JK}$.

    D. $\overline{JK}$ parallel to $\overline{GH}$.

    E. $\overline{JK}$ parallel to $\overline{EF}$.

LESSON 21 GEOMETRY: Congruent Figures and Quadrilaterals

1. Congruent Figures

Two figures are **congruent** if they have the same size and shape.

Two line segments are congruent if they have the same length.

Example 1: Which triangles are congruent?

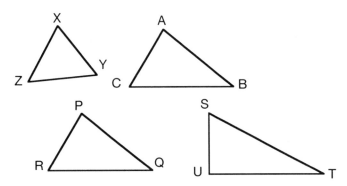

Triangles ABC and PQR are the only triangles that have the same size and shape. The symbol for congruent is ≅, so triangle ABC ≅ triangle PQR.

Example 2: Triangle PQR is congruent to triangle STV. Which line segments are congruent?

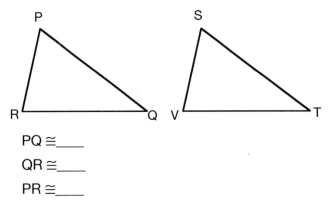

PQ ≅____

QR ≅____

PR ≅____

Congruent line segments have the same length. For two congruent triangles, the sides that "match" are congruent:

PQ ≅ST

QR ≅TV

PR ≅SV

2. <u>Quadrilaterals</u>

A quadrilateral is a figure made up of four sides.

<u>COMMON QUADRILATERALS</u>

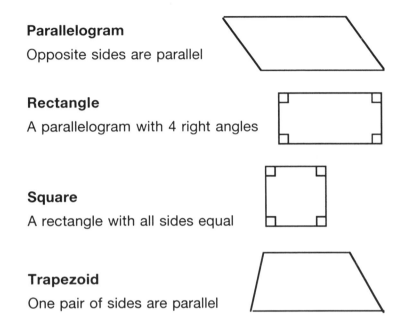

Parallelogram
Opposite sides are parallel

Rectangle
A parallelogram with 4 right angles

Square
A rectangle with all sides equal

Trapezoid
One pair of sides are parallel

Example 1: Which of these figures is a quadrilateral?

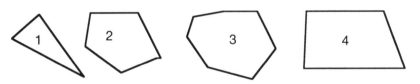

Figure number 4 is a quadrilateral, since it has four sides.

Example 2: Which of the following is a trapezoid?

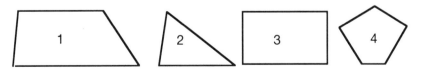

Figure number 1 is a trapezoid, since it is a quadrilateral with a pair of sides parallel.

PRACTICE

1. Which two shapes are congruent? Choose the numbers of the figures. _____

(**_Hint:_** Identical twins are still identical even when one is standing up and the other is lying down)

2. Which two shapes are congruent? Choose the numbers of the figures. _____

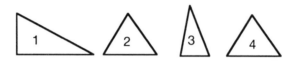

3. Which figure below is a square? Choose the number of the figure. _____

4. Which figure below is a trapezoid? Choose the number of the figure. _____

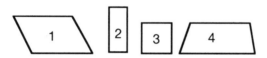

5. Which figure is a parallelogram, but not a rectangle?
   Choose the number of the figure. _____

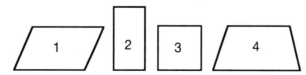

Choose the correct answer for Questions 6-9.

6. Which two shapes are congruent?

 A.

 B.

 C.

 D.

 E.

7. Which shape is a square?

A.

B.

C.

D.

E.

8. Select the pair of sides of the two triangles that are congruent to each other.

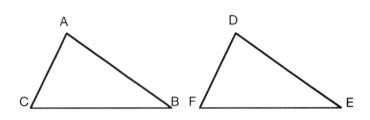

A. BC ≅ DF
B. BC ≅ DE
C. AB ≅ DE
D. AB ≅ EF
E. AC ≅ DE

(**_Hint:_** The symbol ≅ means "is congruent to".)

9. Select the sides of the triangles that are congruent to each other.

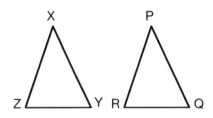

A. YZ ≅ PR
B. YZ ≅ PQ
C. XY ≅ QR
D. XZ ≅ PR
E. XZ ≅ PQ

LESSON 22   GEOMETRY:
Parts of Circles

A **circle** is made up of all points that are the same distance from a fixed point.

There are five key parts of a circle.

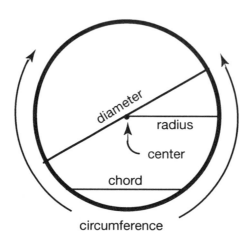

The fixed point is called the **center** of the circle.

The **circumference** of a circle is the distance around the circle.

A **diameter** is a line segment that passes through the center of the circle and has endpoints on the circle.

A **radius** is a line segment from the center of the circle to any point on the circle. The radius is 1/2 the diameter of the circle.

A **chord** is a line segment that connects any two points on the circle.

Example 1: In this drawing of a circle, what part of the circle are $\overline{XY}, \overline{PQ},$ and $\overline{OP}$?

$\overline{XY}$ is a line segment that has endpoints on the circle and that passes through the center of the circle. So $\overline{XY}$ is a *diameter*.

$\overline{PQ}$ Is a line segment connecting two points of the circle. So $\overline{PQ}$ is a *chord*.

$\overline{OP}$ Is a segment from the center of the circle to a point on the circle. $\overline{OP}$ is a *radius*.

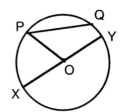

-64-

PRACTICE

1. In the drawing, what part of the circle is $\overline{AB}$?

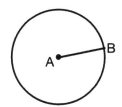

   A. center

   B. radius

   C. diameter

   D. circumference

   E. chord

2. In the drawing, what part of the circle is $\overline{XY}$?

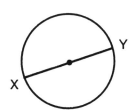

   A. center

   B. radius

   C. diameter

   D. circumference

   E. edge

3. In the drawing, what part of the circle is Q?

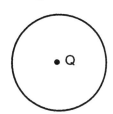

   A. chord

   B. radius

   C. diameter

   D. circumference

   E. center

4. Line segment $\overline{XZ}$ is a

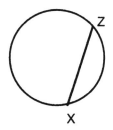

   A. chord

   B. radius

   C. diameter

   D. circumference

   E. center

5. If the radius of a circle is 15 in., then
how long is the diameter?

    A. 7.5 in.

    B. 15 in.

    C. 20 in.

    D. 25 in.

    E. 30 in.

6. Which circle is shown with a diameter?

    A.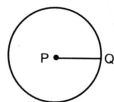

    B.

    C.

    D.

    E.

7. Line segment $\overline{PQ}$ is a

    A. radius

    B. circumference

    C. diameter

    D. center

    E. chord

8. Line segment $\overline{GH}$ is a

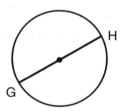

    A. radius

    B. circumference

    C. diameter

    D. center

    E. diagonal

9. Which circle is shown with a chord
drawn?

    A.

    B.

    C.

    D.

    E.

10. If the diameter of a circle is 40 cm,
then how long is the radius?

    A. 10 cm

    B. 20 cm

    C. 30 cm

    D. 60 cm

    E. 80 cm

LESSON 23   GEOMETRY: Three-Dimensional Figures

Three-dimensional figures are not flat figures. They have length, width, and height. Some common three-dimensional figures are cubes, rectangular prisms (boxes), pyramids, cylinders, and cones.

1. Rectangular Prisms

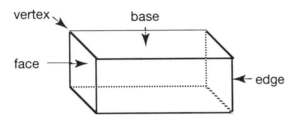

RECTANGULAR PRISM: all sides are rectangles. *Example*: box

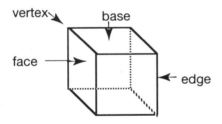

CUBE: all sides are squares. A cube is a special kind of rectangular prism. *Example*: blocks children play with.

The sides, top, and bottom of both these figures are called **faces**.

The *top* and *bottom* faces are also called **bases**.

The faces meet at **edges**.

The edges meet at **vertices** (plural of **vertex**).

Example 1: How many faces does a rectangular prism (a box) have?

Look at one of the figures above. They are both rectangular prisms.

The top and bottom are *faces*. There are 2 faces on the left and right.

There are also 2 more faces in front and back. That's 6 faces altogether.

All rectangular prisms have 6 faces.

-67-

2. <u>Other Three-Dimensional Figures</u>

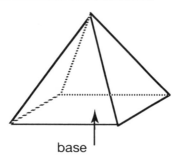

base

<u>PYRAMID</u>: the base is often a square. The other faces are triangles.

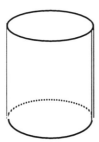

<u>CYLINDER</u>: The top and bottom bases are circles. *Example*: a can.

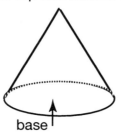

base

<u>CONE</u>: The base is a circle. *Example*: an ice cream cone;.

<u>SPHERE</u>: *Example*: a ball

<u>*Example 1:*</u> Name two three-dimensional figures whose bottoms are circles.

Look at the diagrams above. You will see that the bottoms of the cylinder and cone are circles.

PRACTICE

Write the name of each figure.

1. _____

2. _____

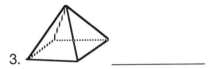

3. _____

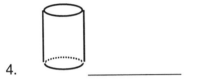

4. _____

5. _____

6. _____

7. _____

Choose the correct answer for Questions 8-12.

8. Which figure has circles for the top and bottom?

    A. pyramid

    B. cylinder

    C. sphere

    D. cube

    E. cone

9. Which figure has 6 faces that are all squares?

    A. pyramid

    B. cylinder

    C. sphere

    D. cube

    E. cone

10. How many edges does a rectangular prism have?

    A. 6

    B. 8

    C. 10

    D. 12

    E. 14

11. Which figure comes to a point on one end?

    A. rectangular prism

    B. cylinder

    C. sphere

    D. cube

    E. cone

12. Which figure looks like a ball?

    A. pyramid

    B. cylinder

    C. sphere

    D. cube

    E. cone

LESSON 24   GEOMETRY AND MEASUREMENT: Perimeter

A **polygon** is a closed figure made up of straight sides. Examples of polygons are triangles, square, rectangles, parallelograms, hexagons (6 sides), and octagons (8 sides).

The **_perimeter_** of a polygon is the distance around the polygon.

To find the perimeter, add the lengths of the sides.

These are the perimeter formulas you need to know:

Triangle: $p = a + b + c$ (where p = perimeter and a, b, and c are the sides)

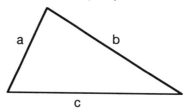

Square: $p = 4s$ (where s = side)

Rectangle: $p = 2L + 2W$ (where L = length and W = width)

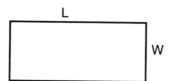

Example 1: Find the perimeter of a rectangle that is 10 feet long and 5 feet wide.

Step 1. Use the formula for the perimeter of a rectangle:

$$p = 2L + 2W$$

Step 2. Substitute 10 for L and 5 for W in the formula:

$$L = 10 \text{ and } W = 5$$
$$p = 2(10) + 2(5)$$
$$p = 20 + 10$$
$$p = 30 \text{ feet}$$

PRACTICE

Find the perimeter of each figure in Questions 1-3.

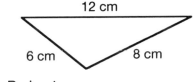

1. Perimeter = _____

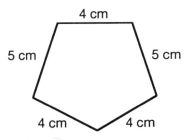

2. Perimeter = _____

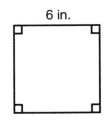

3. Perimeter = _____

For Questions 4-10, choose the correct answer.

4. The perimeter of a square is 80 cm. What is the length of each side of the square?

    A. 5 cm

    B. 10 cm

    C. 12 cm

    D. 15 cm

    E. 20 cm

5. What is the perimeter of a rectangular room whose length is 22 ft and whose width is 15 ft?

    A. 40 ft

    B. 50 ft

    C. 74 ft

    D. 80 ft

    E. 84 ft

6. What is the perimeter of a triangle with sides equal to 9 in., 12 in., and 15 in.?

    A. 36 in.

    B. 40 in.

    C. 45 in.

    D. 48 in.

    E. 52 in.

7. Which is the formula for the perimeter of a rectangle?

    A. $p = 2L + W$

    B. $p = L + 2W$

    C. $p = L + W$

    D. $p = 2L + 2W$

    E. $p = 3L + 2W$

8. Each side of a square lot is 40 ft. If you wanted to fence the lot, how much fencing would you need?

    A. 40 ft

    B. 60 ft

    C. 80 ft

    D. 100 ft

    E. 160 ft

9. The perimeter of a square is 36 cm. What is the length of each side?

    A. 4 cm

    B. 6 cm

    C. 8 cm

    D. 9 cm

    E. 12 cm

10. The distance around a pentagon (5 sides) with all sides equal in length is 40 cm. What is the length of each side?

    A. 6 cm

    B. 8 cm

    C. 10 cm

    D. 12 cm

    E. 15 cm

LESSON 25 GEOMETRY AND MEASUREMENT: Area

1. Finding the Area of a Region

Area is the amount of surface of something. It is usually measured in square units.

Example 1: What is the area of the shaded part of the diagram? (Each square of the grid equals 1 square centimeter.)

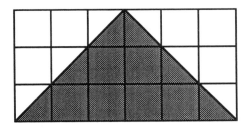

Step 1. Count the number of shaded full squares: 6

Step 2. Count the number of shaded half-squares: 6

Step 3. Compute the area of the shaded half-squares:

6 half-squares = $6 \times \frac{1}{2}$ = 3 square centimeters

Step 4. Add the full squares and the half-squares:

$$
\begin{array}{ll}
6 \text{ full squares} & = 6 \text{ square centimeters} \\
+ \ 6 \text{ half squares} & = 3 \text{ square centimeters} \\
\hline
\text{Area} & = 9 \text{ square centimeters}
\end{array}
$$

2. Formulas for Area

You need to know the formulas for the area of a square and rectangle.

Square: $A = s^2$ (s^2 means s x s)

(A = area and s = side)

Rectangle: $A = LW$

(where L = length and W = width)

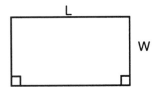

-73-

Remember: if you measure length in feet, then you measure area in **square** feet. If you measure length in centimeters, then you measure area in **square** centimeters.

> **_Example 1:_** Find the area of a rectangle that is 40 feet long and 20 feet wide.
>
> Use the formula: A = LW
>
> Substitute L = 40 and W = 20 in the formula
>
> A = 40 x 20 = 800
>
> The area of the rectangle is 800 square feet.

PRACTICE

1. All the small triangles below are the same size. Which figure has the greatest area?

A.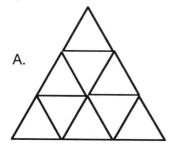

B.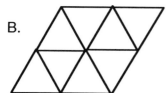

C.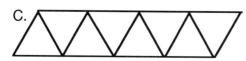

D.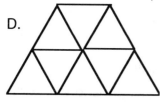

E.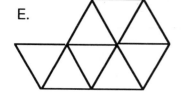

2. Find the area of the shaded portion of the diagram. Each square of the grid is a square centimeter.

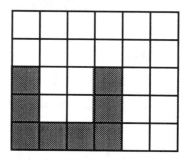

A. 6 square centimeters

B. 7 square centimeters

C. 8 square centimeters

D. 9 square centimeters

E. 10 square centimeters

3. Which formula is for the area of a square?

A. $A = \frac{1}{2}bh$

B. $A = 2LW$

C. $A = 4s$

D. $A = 2L + 2W$

E. $A = s^2$

4. Find the area of the shaded portion of the diagram. Each square of the grid is a square centimeter.

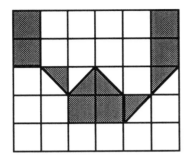

A. $6\frac{1}{2}$ square centimeters

B. 7 square centimeters

C. $7\frac{1}{2}$ square centimeters

D. 8 square centimeters

E. $8\frac{1}{2}$ square centimeters

5. Which formula is for the area of a rectangle?

A. $A = \frac{1}{2}bh$

B. $A = LW$

C. $A = 4s$

D. $A = 2L + 2W$

E. $A = s^2$

Find the area of each figure in Questions 6-9.

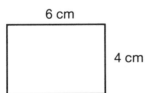

6.

A. 12 square centimeters

B. 14 square centimeters

C. 18 square centimeters

D. 24 square centimeters

E. 30 square centimeters

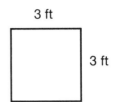

7.

A. 9 square feet

B. 12 square feet

C. 15 square feet

D. 18 square feet

E. 24 square feet

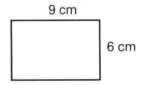

8.

A. 15 square centimeters

B. 24 square centimeters

C. 30 square centimeters

D. 45 square centimeters

E. 54 square centimeters

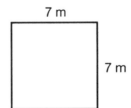

9.

A. 9 square meters

B. 24 square meters

C. 36 square meters

D. 45 square meters

E. 49 square meters

LESSON 26 GEOMETRY AND MEASUREMENT: Volume

In this lesson, you will find the volume of rectangular prisms (boxes). These are the two formulas you should know to find volume (V).

Rectangular prism (box)

V = L x W x H

(L = length, W = width, and H = height)

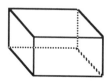

Cube

V = s³ or s x s x s

(s = edge)

Remember, the cube is a special rectangular prism with all three dimensions equal.

Example 1: Nora has a filing cabinet that is 3 feet long, 2 feet wide, and 4 feet high. What is the volume of the cabinet?

Step 1. Use the formula for the volume of a rectangular prism:

V = L x W x H

Step 2. Substitute number in the formula and solve:

V = 3 x 2 x 4

V = 24 cu ft

The volume of the filing cabinet is 24 cu ft.

PRACTICE

In Questions 1-4 you are given the dimensions of rectangular prisms. Find the volume of each prism. Make sure you write the units.

1. L = 10 cm, W = 10 cm, H = 5 cm   V = _____

2. L = 8 m, W = 7 m, H = 4 m   V = _____

3. L = 3 ft, W = 2 ft, H = 8 ft   V = _____

4. L = 10 in., W = 8 in., H = 4 in.   V = _____

In Questions 5-6, you are given the edge of cubes. Find the volume of each cube. Make sure you write the units.

5. s = 6 in.　　V = _____

6. s = 12 cm　V = _____

Choose the correct answers for Questions 8-10.

7. What is the volume of the rectangular prism shown in the diagram?

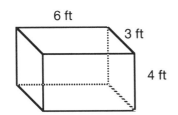

A. 12 cu. ft
B. 24 cu. ft
C. 36 cu. ft
D. 60 cu. ft
E. 72 cu. ft

8. What is the volume of the rectangular prism shown in the diagram?

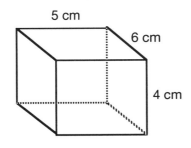

A. 140 cu. cm
B. 130 cu. cm
C. 120 cu. cm
D. 100 cu. cm
E. 80 cu. cm

9. What is the volume of a cube with edges equal to 10 ft?
A. 30 cu. ft
B. 100 cu. ft
C. 500 cu. ft
D. 1000 cu. ft
E. 10,000 cu. ft

10. Jill's new office is a cube: each edge is 14 ft. What is the volume of this room?
A. 14 cu. ft
B. 169 cu. ft
C. 196 cu. ft
D. 2744 cu. ft
E. 2888 cu. ft

LESSON 27   DATA COLLECTION AND ANALYSIS: Probability and Combinations

1. Probability

The **probability** of an event tells us the likelihood that an event will take place. Probability is always a ratio between 0 and 1. (We use the letter p to stand for *probability*.)

Example 1: What is the probability that the spinner will stop at a section marked B if you spin it?

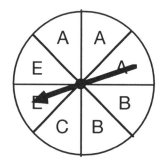

Step 1. Note the number of equal sections of the spinner (total *possible outcomes*):

The spinner is divided into 8 sections.

Step 2. Find the number of sections marked B (total *favorable outcomes*):

There are 2 sections marked B.

Step 3. Set up this ratio (this is the probability):

$$p = \frac{\text{favorable outcomes}}{\text{possible outcomes}} = \frac{2}{8}$$

Step 4. Reduce the fraction to lowest terms, if necessary.

$$p = \frac{2}{8} = \frac{1}{4}$$

The probability of the spinner stopping at B is $\frac{1}{4}$.

Example 2: If 35% of the students at Maple Avenue School walk to school, what is the probability that a student chosen at random walks to school?

Percent means part of 100, so 35% is the same as $\frac{35}{100}$.

Reduce the fraction: $\frac{35}{100} = \frac{7}{20}$.

The probability that a student walks to school is 7/20.

Example 3: Seven out of 10 students voted to have a longer lunch break. If a student is chosen at random, then what is the probability of choosing a student who did NOT vote to have a longer lunch break?

If you add the probability of something happening to the probability of its NOT happening, the sum must equal 1.

The probability of choosing a student who voted "YES" is $\frac{7}{10}$.

Subtract this fraction from the number 1 to find the probability of choosing a student who voted "NO":

$$1 - \frac{7}{10} = \frac{3}{10}$$

So the probability of choosing a student who did NOT vote for the longer lunch break is $\frac{3}{10}$.

2. Combinations

Example 1: Tammy has four dresses and three blouses. How many combinations of dresses and blouses can she wear?

To find the number of different combinations, multiply:

(number of dresses) x (number of blouses)

$$4 \times 3 = 12$$

Tammy could wear 12 different combinations of dresses and blouses.

PRACTICE

Choose the correct answers.

1. There are nine cards in a bag, numbered 1 through 9. What is the probability of choosing the card with the number 5?

    A. $\frac{1}{9}$

    B. $\frac{1}{6}$

    C. $\frac{4}{9}$

    D. $\frac{5}{6}$

    E. $\frac{9}{5}$

2. What is the probability of rolling a 4 on a single roll of a die (one of a pair of dice)? (***Hint***: A die is a cube and has 6 faces.)

    A. $\frac{3}{2}$

    B. $\frac{2}{6}$

    C. $\frac{1}{6}$

    D. $\frac{1}{5}$

    E. $\frac{1}{4}$

3. What is the probability that the spinner will stop in a shaded area if you spin it?

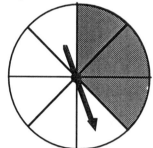

A. $\frac{1}{8}$

B. $\frac{1}{4}$

C. $\frac{2}{8}$

D. $\frac{3}{8}$

E. $\frac{3}{9}$

4. If you pick a shape at random, what is the probability of picking a triangle?

□ △ □ □

A. 1 out of 3

B. 1 out of 4

C. 2 out of 3

D. 4 out of 4

E. 3 out of 4

5. A bag contains cards with the numbers 1 through 9. What is the probability that an even number will be chosen on a single draw of a card?

A. $\frac{1}{9}$

B. $\frac{2}{9}$

C. $\frac{4}{9}$

D. $\frac{5}{9}$

E. $\frac{2}{3}$

6. What is the probability that if you spin the spinner it will stop at a section marked T?

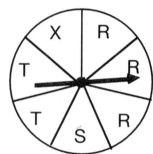

A. $\frac{1}{7}$

B. $\frac{2}{7}$

C. $\frac{3}{7}$

D. $\frac{2}{6}$

E. $\frac{2}{5}$

7. What is the probability of getting a tails on a single toss of a coin?

A. $\frac{1}{2}$

B. $\frac{1}{3}$

C. $\frac{1}{4}$

D. $\frac{1}{5}$

E. $\frac{1}{6}$

8. A bag has 10 marbles in it. If 2 marbles are blue, 4 are red, and 4 are yellow, what is the probability that if you pick one marble from bag, it will be red?

A. $\frac{2}{5}$

B. $\frac{3}{10}$

C. $\frac{1}{5}$

D. 4

E. 10

9. Donna's name is one of 15 names in a hat. If a single name is be picked at random from the hat, what is the probability that her name will be the one that is picked?

    A. $\frac{2}{3}$

    B. $\frac{1}{2}$

    C. $\frac{1}{3}$

    D. $\frac{1}{14}$

    E. $\frac{1}{15}$

10. If Juan gets to class on time 90% of the time, what is the probability that he will get to class on time next time?

    A. 90

    B. 0.1

    C. 0.3

    D. 0.8

    E. 0.9

11. If the probability that it will rain is 60%, then what is the probability that it will NOT rain? (**_Hint_**: Remember that the probabilities of something happening and something not happening must add to 1.)

    A. 10%

    B. 20%

    C. 30%

    D. 40%

    E. 60%

12. A box has 9 blocks in it: 2 are blue; 3 are purple; 1 is red; 2 are green; and 1 is yellow. If you shake up the box and pull out only 1 block without looking, what color will it most likely be?

    A. blue

    B. purple

    C. red

    D. green

    E. yellow

13. The menu for the Madison Plaza Restaurant shows 5 main courses and 3 desserts. How many combinations of main courses and desserts can be made?

    A. 3

    B. 5

    C. 8

    D. 10

    E. 15

14. Sally can pick from 7 pens and 3 notebooks to do her work. How many combinations of pens and notebooks can she make?

    A. 21

    B. 14

    C. 10

    D. 7

    E. 3

15. Nine of 10 students from Riverview School ride the bus to school. If a student is chosen at random from Riverview School, what is the probability of choosing a student who does NOT ride the bus to school? (**Hint**: Remember that the probability of a student riding the bus and the probability of a student not riding the bus must add to 1.)

    A. 10%

    B. 20%

    C. 50%

    D. 80%

    E. 90%

16. If a penny is tossed 100 times, it is most likely that the number of tails will be— (**Hint**: Multiply the probability of tails by the number of tosses.)

    A. close to 50.

    B. close to 40.

    C. close to 30.

    D. close to 20.

    E. close to 10.

17. Smith rolls 30 dice. How many will probably come up showing 3? (**Hint**: A die has 6 sides.)

    A. 20

    B. 15

    C. 10

    D. 6

    E. 5

18. If one coin is selected from a box containing a penny, nickel, dime, and quarter, what is the probability that it will be worth more than 15 cents?

    A. $\frac{1}{5}$

    B. $\frac{1}{4}$

    C. $\frac{2}{5}$

    D. $\frac{2}{4}$

    E. $\frac{1}{2}$

19. If you spin this spinner a hundred times, where will it most likely stop the least often?

    A. at 1

    B. at 2

    C. at 3

    D. at 4

    E. at 5

LESSON 28 DATA COLLECTION AND ANALYSIS: Tables

1. Tables

A table contains information or data, usually in numerical form.

Example 1: This is a weekly schedule for Terry's soccer team:

	Mon	Tu	Wed	Thurs	Fri	Sat
Practice	3:00	3:30	3:30	3:00	3:45	
Meeting		5:00		5:00		
Game						10:30

How many days does the team practice before 3:30?

  Step 1. Find the row for practice:

  This row has these times: 3:00, 3:30, 3:30, 3:00, and 3:45.

  Step 2. Count the number of times before 3:30:

  There are two practices before 3:30, on Monday and Thursday.

PRACTICE

Use this table to answer Questions 1-3.

NUMBER OF BOOKS READ BY STUDENTS LAST WEEK

	Mon	Tu	Wed	Thurs	Fri
Class 6-1	2	3	5	0	2
Class 6-2	1	4	1	3	2
Class 6-3	3	2	0	3	5

1. How many books did Class 6-2 read last week? _____

2. How many more books did Class 6-3 read than Class 6-1 last week? _____

3. How many books did the three classes read on Wednesday? _____

-83-

Use this table to answer Questions 4-6. Choose the correct answer for each.

NUMBER OF POINTS VERONICA SCORED IN BASKETBALL GAMES

Game	1	2	3	4	5	6	7	8	9	10
Points Scored	8	12	16	14	10	7	9	16	22	14

4. How many times did Veronica score more than 15 points?

A. 1
B. 2
C. 3
D. 4
E. 5

5. How many times did Veronica score less than 10 points?

A. 1
B. 2
C. 3
D. 4
E. 5

6. Which statement is false?

A. Veronica scored more points in the last three games than she did in the first three games.
B. She scored the most in game 9.
C. She scored the least in game 6.
D. She scored more in game 8 than she did in game 3.
E. She scored more in game 10 than in game 1.

Use this table to answer Questions 7-9. Choose the correct answer for each.

NUMBER OF ERRORS KATHY MADE ON SPELLING TESTS

Test Number	1	2	3	4	5	6	7	8
Number of Errors	4	5	3	2	8	6	1	5

7. How many times did Kathy make more than 5 errors?

A. 1
B. 2
C. 3
D. 4
E. 5

8. How many times did Kathy make less than 5 errors?

A. 1
B. 2
C. 3
D. 4
E. 5

9. How many times did Kathy make 5 errors?

  A. 1
  B. 2
  C. 3
  D. 4
  E. 5

10. According to the chart below, how much is the tax on $.75?

Amount of Sale	Tax
$.08 – .21	$.01
.22 – .35	.02
.36 – .49	.03
.50 – .64	.04
.65 – .78	.05
.79 –. 92	.06

  A. $.06
  B. $.05
  C. $.04
  D. $.03
  E. None of the above

LESSON 29   DATA COLLECTION AND ANALYSIS: Graphs

1. Bar Graphs

In a bar graph, the bars tell you the amounts in different categories.

Example 1: This bar graph shows the amount of money collected to help build a children's zoo. How much money was collected from the 3rd, 5th, and 7th graders altogether?

MONEY COLLECTED TO HELP BUILD CHILDREN'S ZOO

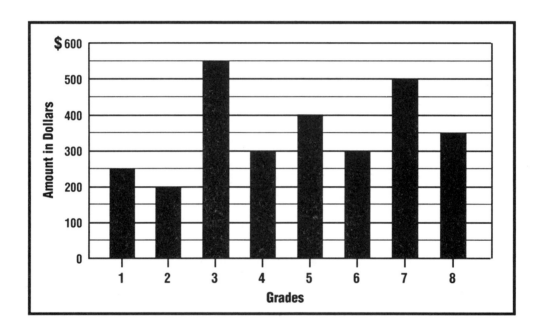

Step 1. Find the bars for Grades 3, 5, and 7.

Step 2. Go to the tops of the bars for these three grades.

Step 3. Move left from the tops of the three bars to the scale numbers. (It helps to use your finger.)

Step 4. Write the three scale numbers for the three grades:

$\qquad$ Grade 3—$550

$\qquad$ Grade 5—$400

$\qquad$ Grade 7—$500

Step 5. Add the amounts for the three grades together:

$\qquad$ $550 + $400 + $500 = $1450.

The amount collected from Grades 3, 5, and 7 was $1450.

2. Line Graphs

In a line graph, a line connects dots to show a trend.

Example 1: This line graph shows the average amounts of TV watched over the weekend by five groups of children. How many more hours of TV did 8-year olds watch than 6-year olds?

NUMBER OF HOURS OF TV WATCHED OVER WEEKENDS

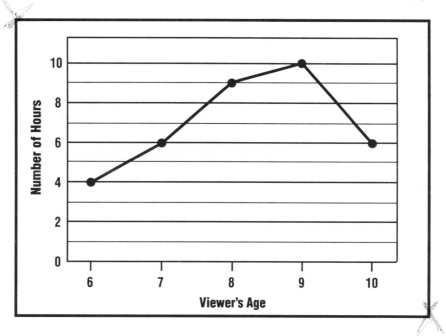

Step 1. Find Age 6.

Step 2. Go up along the Age 6 line to the dot.

Step 3. Move left to the scale opposite this dot.

Step 4. Read the scale number:

   The scale number is 4 hours.

Step 5. Repeat Steps 1, 2, 3, and 4 for Age 8.

   The scale number is 9 hours.

Step 6. Subtract: 9 hours - 4 hours = 5 hours

8-year olds watched 5 hours more TV over the weekend than 6-year olds did.

3. Pictographs

In a pictograph, a picture represents a number.

> ***Example 1:*** How many musical instruments are in School 5?

NUMBER OF MUSICAL INSTRUMENTS IN THE SCHOOLS

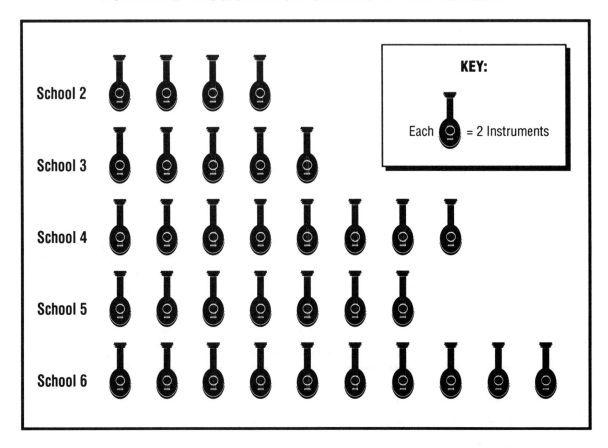

Look at the information at the top of the graph. It tells you that each musical instrument symbol stands for **2** instruments, not just 1.

School 5 has 7 symbols, so we multiply by 2:

$$7 \times 2 = 14$$

There are 14 musical instruments in School 5.

PRACTICE

Use this bar graph to answer Questions 1-3. Choose the correct answer for each.

NUMBER OF BOOKS READ THIS MONTH BY SIXTH-GRADE CLASSES

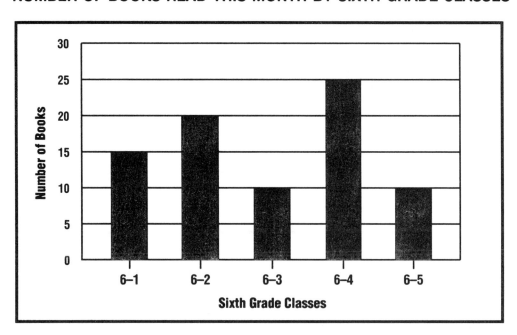

1. How many books did Class 6-5 read during the month?

    A. 5

    B. 10

    C. 15

    D. 20

    E. 25

2. How many more books did Class 6-4 read than did Class 6-2?

    A. 5

    B. 10

    C. 15

    D. 20

    E. 25

3. Altogether, how many books did Classes 6-1 and 6-5 read this month?

    A. 5

    B. 10

    C. 15

    D. 20

    E. 25

Use this line graph to answer Questions 4-6. Choose the correct answer.

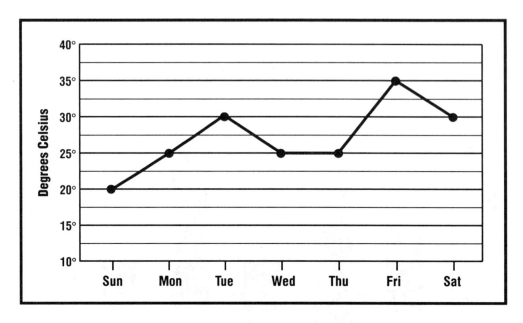

TEMPERATURE LAST WEEK OUTSIDE CARMEN'S CLASSROOM

4. What was the temperature on Tuesday?

    A. 15° C

    B. 20° C

    C. 25° C

    D. 30° C

    E. 35° C

5. What was the difference in temperature between Monday and Thursday?

    A. 20° C

    B. 15° C

    C. 10° C

    D. 5° C

    E. 0° C

6. What was the difference in temperature between Friday and Saturday?

    A. 5° C

    B. 10° C

    C. 15° C

    D. 20° C

    E. 25° C

Use this pictograph to answer Questions 7-9. Choose the correct answer for each.

NUMBER OF CARTONS OF MILK SOLD IN SCHOOL CAFETERIA

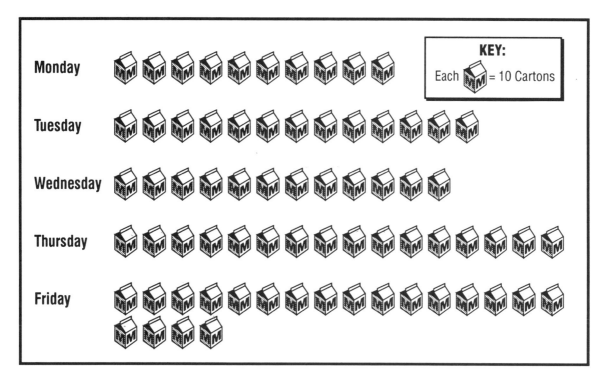

7. How many cartons were sold on

   Tuesday?

   A. 10

   B. 13

   C. 100

   D. 130

   E. 160

8. How many cartons were sold on

   Wednesday?

   A. 10

   B. 12

   C. 100

   D. 110

   E. 120

9. How many more cartons were sold on

   Friday than on Thursday?

   A. 10

   B. 20

   C. 30

   D. 40

   E. 50

Use this bar graph to answer Question 10.

TEMPERATURE AT NOON IN SMITHVILLE

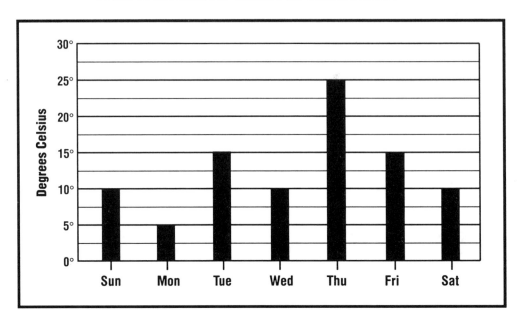

10. When did the temperature change the most?

    A. Sunday to Thursday

    B. Monday to Tuesday

    C. Monday to Thursday

    D. Wednesday to Thursday

    E. Thursday to Friday

LESSON 30   DATA COLLECTION AND ANALYSIS: Mean and Median

1. The Mean

To find the **mean** (or **average**) of a group of numbers, follow these two steps.

Step 1. Add the numbers.

Step 2. Divide the sum of Step 1 by the number of numbers in the group.

$$\textbf{\textit{Mean}} \text{ of a set of numbers} = \frac{\text{sum of all numbers}}{\text{number of numbers}}$$

Example 1: These were the temperatures at noon last week. What was the mean temperature?

Day	Temperature (°F)
Monday	44
Tuesday	51
Wednesday	52
Thursday	47
Friday	46

Step 1. Add the temperatures:

$44 + 51 + 52 + 47 + 46 = 240$

Step 2. Divide by the number of days:

$240 \div 5 = 48$

The mean temperature is 48°F.

2. The Median

The **median** is the middle number of a set of numbers arranged in numerical order.

Example 1: The prices of the same computer at five different stores are: $785, $980, $775, $995, and $840. What is the median of these prices?

Step 1. Arrange the prices in order from the lowest to the highest:

$775, $785, $840, $980, $995

Step 2. Pick the amount in the middle:

The middle amount is $840. This is the median.

Note: When you find the median of an <u>even number</u> of pieces of data, then you will have <u>two</u> numbers in the middle. In that case, the median is the <u>mean</u> of those two numbers. Add them and divide by 2.

> **_Example 2:_** Find the median for these numbers:
>
> 25, 14, 19, 25, 22, 29, 19, 24, 28, 21
>
> Arrange the numbers in order from least to greatest:
>
> 14, 19, 19, 21, 22, 24, 25, 25, 28, 29
>
> Since this list has an even number (10) of pieces of data, find the two numbers in the middle. They are 22 and 24.
>
> To find the median, find the **_mean_** of the two middle numbers:
>
> $$\frac{22 + 24}{2} = 23$$
>
> The median is 23.

PRACTICE

Find the mean of these sets of numbers.

1. 25, 25, 25   _____
2. 10, 20, 30, 40, 50   _____
3. 25, 27, 14, 17, 22, 19, 16 _____

Find the median of these numbers:

4. 10, 9, 8, 7, 6,   _____
5. 9, 3, 5, 1, 7, 6, 4, 7, 3   _____
6. 64, 71, 65, 67, 70, 68, 55, 59 _____

(**_Hint_**: See the Note in Section 2, above, just before Example 2.)

Choose the correct answers for these questions.

7. Find the mean and the median of these
   numbers: 22, 29, 24, 21, 19.
   - A. Mean: 23   Median: 21
   - B. Mean: 23   Median: 22
   - C. Mean: 24   Median: 21
   - D. Mean: 24   Median: 22
   - E. Mean: 22   Median: 23

8. Find the mean and the median of
   these numbers: 50, 45, 58, 60, 27.
   - A. Mean: 50   Median: 50
   - B. Mean: 50   Median: 48
   - C. Mean: 52   Median: 50
   - D. Mean: 50   Median: 45
   - E. Mean: 48   Median: 50

9. The temperatures at noon outside
   Larry's bedroom during the past week
   were: 72, 68, 65, 73, 70, 56, and 58.
   What was the mean temperature for
   the week?

   A. 62
   B. 63
   C. 64
   D. 65
   E. 66

10. What is the mean of the following set
    of numbers?

    20, 30, 40, 50, 60

    A. The same as the median of the
       set of numbers.
    B. 30
    C. 50
    D. Less than 20
    E. Greater than 60

11. Another word for *mean* is

    A. average
    B. median
    C. mode
    D. range
    E. deviation

LESSON 31 ESTIMATION: Rounding Numbers

We round numbers when an exact number is not necessary. It is easier to work with rounded numbers.

1. Rounding to the Nearest 10

Example 1: Round 32 to the nearest 10.

Step 1. Place 32 on a number line marked off in intervals of 10:

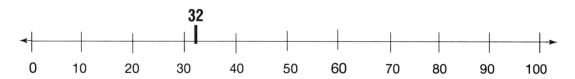

Step 2. Ask: Is 32 closer to 30 or to 40?

32 is closer to 30.

So 32 rounded to the nearest 10 is 30.

Example 2: Round 125 to the nearest 10.

125 is in the middle of the interval between 120 and 130.

Whenever a number is in the middle of an interval of 10, it ends in 5. When this happens, round **up**.

Round 125 **up** to 130.

125 rounded to the nearest 10 is 130.

2. **Rounding to the Nearest 100**

Example 1: Round 568 to the nearest 100.

Step 1. Place 568 on a number line marked off in intervals of 100:

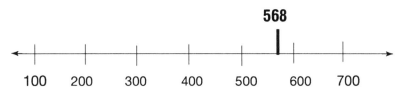

Step 2. Ask: is 568 closer to 500 or to 600?

568 is closer to 600.

568 rounded to the nearest 100 is 600.

Example 2: Round 750 to the nearest 100.

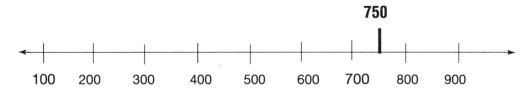

750 is in the middle of the interval between 700 and 800.

When a number is in the middle of an interval of 100, it ends in 50. When this happens, round **up**.

Round 750 **up** to 800.

750 rounded to the nearest 100 is 800.

3. **Rounding to the Nearest 1000**

Example 1: Round 2813 to the nearest 1000.

Place 2813 on a number line marked off in intervals of 1000:

2813 is closer to 3000 than to 2000.

2813 rounded to the nearest 1000 is 3000.

Example 2: Round 4500 to the nearest 1000.

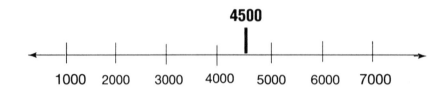

4500 is in the middle of the interval between 4000 and 5000. When a number is in the middle of an interval of 1000, it ends in 500. If this happens, round **up**.

Round 4500 **up** to 5000.

4500 rounded to the nearest 1000 is 5000.

4. Rounding a Decimal Number to the Nearest Whole Number

Example 1: Round 6.4 to the nearest whole number.

Step 1. Place 6.4 on a number line marked off in intervals of 1:

Step 2. Ask: is 6.4 closer to 6 or to 7?

6.4 is closer to 6.

6.4 rounded to the nearest whole number is 6.

Example 2: Round 7.5 to the nearest whole number.

7.5 is in the middle of the interval between 7 and 8. When a decimal in tenths is in the middle of an interval of 1, it ends in .5. When this happens, round **up**.

Round 7.5 **up** to 8.

7.5 rounded to the nearest whole number is 8.

Example 3: Round $215.64 to the nearest dollar.

This amount is between $215 and $216.

64 cents is more than 1/2 dollar, so we round **up** to the next dollar.

$215.64 rounded to the nearest dollar is $216.

PRACTICE

Choose the correct answer for each.

1. Round 46 to the nearest 10.

   A. 4

   B. 40

   C. 45

   D. 50

   E. 55

2. Round 650 to the nearest 100.

   A. 500

   B. 600

   C. 660

   D. 700

   E. 1000

3. Round 2445 to the nearest 1000.

   A. 2000

   B. 2400

   C. 2450

   D. 2500

   E. 3000

4. Round 24.5 to the nearest whole number.

   A. 20

   B. 24

   C. 25

   D. 30

   E. 40

5. Round $78.41 to the nearest dollar.

   A. $70

   B. $75

   C. $78

   D. $79

   E. $90

6. Which of these does not round to 8?

   A. 7.5

   B. 7.7

   C. 8.1

   D. 8.4

   E. 8.5

7. 465 rounded to the nearest 100 is

   A. 400

   B. 450

   C. 460

   D. 490

   E. 500

8. Dana received $37.50 in change when she went shopping. Rounded to the nearest dollar, the change is

   A. $30

   B. $35

   C. $37

   D. $38

   E. $40

9. Jackson said that the distance from his house to school is 22 miles. Rounded to the nearest 10, this distance is
    A. 10 miles
    B. 20 miles
    C. 25 miles
    D. 30 miles
    E. 40 miles

10. The length of a room is 20.5 ft. Rounded to the nearest whole number this length is
    A. 10 ft
    B. 15 ft
    C. 19 ft
    D. 20 ft
    E. 21 ft

11. Norma counted her steps from the front of the building to the swimming pool. She counted 12,451. Round this number to the nearest hundred.
    A. 12,000
    B. 12,400
    C. 12,450
    D. 12,500
    E. 13,000

12. Round sixty-five thousand five hundred seventy-two to the nearest thousand. (Hint: Write the number first.)
    A. 60,000
    B. 64,000
    C. 65,000
    D. 66,000
    E. 70,000

13. Round seven thousand five hundred fifty to the nearest hundred. (Hint: Write the number first.)
    A. 7,000
    B. 7,500
    C. 7,600
    D. 8,000
    E. 8,500

14. Round these numbers to the nearest dollar. Which does not round to $23?
    A. $22.50
    B. $22.75
    C. $22.99
    D. $23.40
    E. $23.50

15. Round these numbers to the nearest dollar. Which number rounds to 14?
    A. 13.1
    B. 13.2
    C. 13.3
    D. 13.4
    E. 13.5

16. Round $7\frac{1}{3}$ to the nearest whole number.
    A. 4
    B. 5
    C. 6
    D. 7
    E. 8

LESSON 32   ESTIMATION: Estimating Answers

We use rounded numbers to make estimates.

Example 1: On his vacation, Stan drove 873 miles on the first day and 624 miles on the second day. Round to the nearest 100 to find about how many miles he drove altogether.

Step 1. Round 873 to the nearest 100:

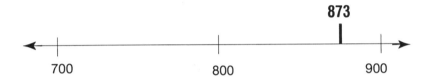

873 rounded to the nearest 100 is 900.

Step 2. Round 624 to the nearest 100:

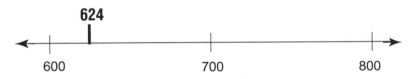

624 rounded to the nearest 100 is 600.

Step 3. Do the math to find how many miles altogether:

Add the rounded numbers:

900 + 600 = 1500

Stan drove about 1500 miles.

Example 2: Estimate this product: 68 x 412.

Round 68 to the nearest 10:

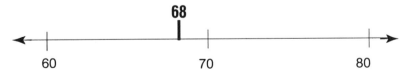

68 rounded to the nearest 10 is 70.

continued

Round 412 to the nearest 100 (NOT the nearest 10. We'll explain why below.):

412

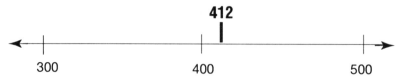

300   400   500

412 rounded to the nearest 100 is 400.

Multiply the rounded numbers: 70 x 400 = 28,000.

28,000 is an estimate for 68 x 412.

Note: In multiplying, as in Example 2, we round each number so that it ends up with only one digit that is NOT zero. That way, the math is easier to do.

PRACTICE

Choose the correct answer for each.

1. Round to the nearest 100 to estimate the sum: 3256 + 2198
   - A. 5000
   - B. 5200
   - C. 5300
   - D. 5400
   - E. 5500

2. Round to the nearest 10 to estimate the answer: 528 - 355
   - A. 200
   - B. 190
   - C. 180
   - D. 170
   - E. 160

3. Round to the nearest 10 to estimate this product: 38 x 41
   - A. 1200
   - B. 1500
   - C. 1600
   - D. 2000
   - E. 2500

4. Round to the nearest 100 to estimate this product: 223 x 831
   - A. 160
   - B. 1600
   - C. 16,000
   - D. 100,000
   - E. 160,000

5. Which is the best estimate for 279 x 61?

    A. 300

    B. 1200

    C. 1800

    D. 2000

    E. 18,000

6. What is the best estimate for 807 x 78?

    A. 64,000

    B. 30,000

    C. 10,000

    D. 6400

    E. 6000

7. Round to the nearest 1000 to find an estimate for 6509 - 3250.

    A. 1000

    B. 2000

    C. 2200

    D. 3000

    E. 4000

LESSON 33 ESTIMATION: Problem Solving

This lesson deals with special types of problems that appear on the Grade 6 IGAP Math Test. Study the examples carefully.

1. Missing Information

When solving problems, make sure you have all the information you need.

Example 1: A soccer team wants to raise $500, so it is selling tickets for a raffle. So far, the team has sold 125 tickets. What additional information is needed to answer this question: how many more tickets does the team have to sell to reach $500?

Step 1. Make sure you know what the problem asks for.

This problem asks us to find out how many more tickets have to be sold.

Step 2. Decide on what you already know.

You already know how many tickets have been sold (125) and how much money ($500) the team wants to make.

Step 3. Ask yourself what is missing.

The missing part is <u>the price of each ticket</u>.

For example, if the tickets cost $1 each, then the team already has $125. But if the tickets cost $2 each, then the team has $250.

2. Extra Information

Sometimes a problem has too much information.

Example 1: Felix spent $65.28 last Wednesday when he went shopping. Yesterday he spent $23.16 at the supermarket, $13.05 at the drug store, and $45.97 at the clothing store. He started with $100. How much money did he have left after shopping yesterday?

What information is not needed to solve this problem? Choose one of these answers.

A. the amount spent on clothing

B. the amount spent at the supermarket

C. the amount spent last Wednesday

D. the amount spent at the drug store

E. the amount started with

To find how much money was left after *yesterday's* shopping trip, we do NOT
need to know about the amount spent *last Wednesday*.

All other amounts listed <u>are</u> needed to solve the problem. So the answer is C.

3. <u>Time-Rate-Distance Problems</u>

Time-rate-distance are common problems in mathematics. These problems frequently
use this formula:

Distance = Time x Rate

D = T x R

Example 1: Tim and Sondra start out on their bicycles from the same place and
travel in opposite directions. Tim travels at 12 miles per hour and Sondra travels at 14
miles per hour. How far apart will they be in 3 hours?

Step 1. Use the formula to compute the distance Tim will travel:

D = T x R

D = 3 x 12

D = 36 miles (Tim's distance)

Step 2. Use the formula to compute the distance Sondra will travel:

D = T x R

D = 3 x 14 = 42 miles (Sondra's distance)

Step 3. Add to find how far apart they are:

42 - 36 = 78 miles

They will be 78 miles apart after 3 hours.

4. <u>Comparison Problems</u>

In a comparison problem you compare two purchases to find which is the better buy.

Example 1: At Ralph's Video the cost of renting 3 videos is $5.40. At Video Visions,
the cost of renting 2 videos is $4. Which is the better buy and why? Choose the
correct answer.

A. Neither—because the cost is the same.

B. Ralph's—because you get more videos.

C. Video Visions—because you spend less money.

D. Ralph's—because you spend 20 cents less for each video.

E. Video Visions—because you spend 20 cents less for each video.

To find the better buy, you have to find the cost of each video. This means dividing the total cost by the number of videos:

$$\text{Cost of each video} = \frac{\text{Total cost}}{\text{Number of videos}}$$

$$\text{Cost of each video at Ralph's} = \frac{\$5.40}{3} = \$1.80$$

$$\text{Cost of each video at Video Visions} = \frac{4}{2} = \$2$$

So the better buy is at Ralph's by 20 cents.
The answer is D.

5. <u>Operations to Solve Problems</u>

The four basic operations are add, subtract, multiply, and divide.
You may be asked which combination of these operations you need to use to solve a problem.

Example 1: You buy 3 pairs of socks at $3.50 a pair. You pay with a 20-dollar bill. Which operations do you perform to find out how much change you should receive?

To solve this problem you need to find the total cost of the 3 pairs of socks, and then find the change.

First, you multiply (3 x $3.50) to find the total cost of the socks.

Then you subtract the total cost from $20 to get the change.

You multiply and subtract.

PRACTICE

Choose the correct answer for each.

1. Mark spent 3 hours and 45 minutes driving to see his friend.

   What additional information do you need to find out at what time he got there?
   - A. the length of time he spent with his friend
   - B. the time he left on his trip
   - C. the time he returned home
   - D. the place where his friend lives
   - E. the route he took to get there

2. Harold is 11 years old. His birthday is on September 9. Sam is twice as old as Kathy. Kathy is 3 years younger than Jack. Jack is the same age as Harold. You want to know how old Sam is.

   What information is NOT needed to solve this problem?
   - A. Harold is 11 years old.
   - B. Harold's birthday is on September 9.
   - C. Sam is twice as old as Kathy.
   - D. Kathy is 3 years younger than Jack.
   - E. Jack is the same age as Harold.

3. Karl and Joan walk towards each other from opposite ends of a walking trail. Karl walks at 3 miles per hour and Joan walks at 4 miles per hour. If they meet in 3 hours, how long is the trail?
   - A. 11 miles
   - B. 13 miles
   - C. 15 miles
   - D. 18 miles
   - E. 21 miles

4. Lunch for Tony and his two friends came to $18.56 plus tax of $1.11. If the three of them spit the total cost equally, which operations do you perform to find out how much each had to pay?
   - A. add and multiply
   - B. multiply and divide
   - C. multiply and add
   - D. add and divide
   - E. add and subtract

5. What is the mystery number (N) that satisfies these clues?

$$N < 20$$
$$N > 4 + 7$$

N is even

N is a multiple of 8

A. 10

B. 12

C. 14

D. 16

E. 18

6. Denise bought $1.25 worth of apples. Barbara bought $\frac{1}{2}$ pound of apples. Which girl bought more apples?

A. Denise

B. Barbara. She bought twice as much.

C. They bought the same amount.

D. Barbara. She bought $\frac{1}{2}$ as much.

E. You can't tell who bought more.

7. Juana scored a total of 128 points for her basketball team last season. What additional information do you need to determine the average number of points she scored per game?

A. how long the season was

B. the number of points her team made during the season

C. the number of games she played

D. the number of games her team lost

E. the number of games her team won

8. Andrés sold his bicycle for $250. What additional information do you need to find out how much profit he made?

A. the price he paid for the bike

B. the price advertised in the newspaper

C. the price of the bike when new

D. the amount of tax he paid for the bike

E. the length of time he owned the bike

9. What is the mystery number (N) that satisfies these clues?

$$N < 40$$
$$N > 30 - 10$$

N is even

N is a multiple of 7

A. 14

B. 21

C. 28

D. 30

E. 35

10. Red pencils cost 3 for 20 cents. Blue pencils cost 10 cents each, and yellow ones cost 2 for 15 cents. Find the total cost of 6 red and 6 yellow pencils. (**_Hint_**: This is an example of a problem with too much information.)

A. 85 cents

B. 75 cents

C. 65 cents

D. 50 cents

E. 35 cents

11. Norma bought 2 magazines at $3 each and 4 magazines at $2 each. How much did the magazines cost?

    A. $16

    B. $14

    C. $12

    D. $10

    E. $8

12. The area of the walls in Natali's living room is about 2000 square feet. A gallon of paint will cover about 400 square feet and costs $11. Which operations would you perform to find out how much the cost of painting the walls would be?

    A. add and multiply

    B. divide and multiply

    C. divide and add

    D. multiply and add

    E. multiply and add

13. Look back at Question 12. How much will it cost Natali to paint the walls of her living room?

    A. $33

    B. $44

    C. $55

    D. $55

    E. $66

LESSON 34   TEST TAKING TIPS:
Tips on Taking the IGAP Math Test

The IGAP Math test consists of 70 <u>multiple-choice</u> questions. For each question, you are given 5 possible answers. You have to choose the correct answer from among these 5 possibilities. There is only one answer to each question.

The test is a <u>timed</u> test. This means you have a fixed amount of time to take the test. The test is divided into two 40-minute parts of 35 questions each.

Here are some tips that will help when you take the test:

- ***Read each question carefully.*** Make sure you understand the question before you start to work it out.

- ***Try to work as carefully as you can.*** Write down everything that can help you, even the most obvious thing. Don't leave anything to chance.

- ***Make sure you answer the question that is asked.*** For example, if a question asks for the <u>least</u> number, make sure you find the least, not the greatest number. If the question asks for the <u>perimeter</u>, make sure you find the perimeter, not the area.

- ***Ask yourself if the answer makes sense.***

    When you find the answer, ask yourself if the answer is a reasonable answer to the question.

- ***If you cannot find the answer, make an "educated guess" at the answer.***

    Use the answers given—ask yourself which one makes the most sense. Remember, there is no penalty for incorrect answers.

- ***Answer as many questions as you can.***

    Move along from one question to the next. Don't spend a long time on any one question.

- ***Use every minute of the test to get the highest score possible.***

Use these tips as you take the Practice Test in the next section.

PRACTICE TEST

IGAP MATHEMATICS COACH
Grade 6
PART 1

Answer each of the following questions.

1. How do you say the number 2350?

    A. two thousand, three hundred

    B. two thousand, two hundred fifty

    C. two thousand, three hundred fifty

    D. three thousand, two hundred fifty

    E. three thousand, two hundred

2. How do you say the number 3,460,300?

    A. three million, four hundred sixty thousand, six hundred

    B. three million, four thousand, three hundred

    C. three million, four hundred sixty thousands, three

    D. three million, six hundred forty thousand, three hundred

    E. three million, four hundred sixty thousand, three hundred

3. Change $2\frac{3}{8}$ to an improper fraction.

    A. $\frac{16}{8}$

    B. $\frac{19}{8}$

    C. $\frac{21}{8}$

    D. $\frac{19}{3}$

    E. $\frac{16}{3}$

4. What is another way to write $\frac{3}{4} + 5\frac{1}{6}$?

    A. $\frac{3}{4} + \frac{31}{5}$

    B. $\frac{3}{4} + \frac{31}{6}$

    C. $\frac{3}{4} + \frac{30}{5}$

    D. $\frac{3}{4} + \frac{30}{5}$

    E. $\frac{3}{4} + \frac{32}{6}$

5. There are 32 students in Stan's class. If one-fourth of them take a bus to school, how many take a bus to school?

    A. 6

    B. 8

    C. 10

    D. 12

    E. 16

6. Felicia watched 30 hours of video movies last week. One-sixth of the time she watched movies she has seen before. How many hours did she watch movies she has seen before?

    A. 3

    B. 4

    C. 5

    D. 6

    E. 8

7. Which fraction is the largest?

A. $\frac{1}{6}$

B. $\frac{2}{5}$

C. $\frac{3}{7}$

D. $\frac{1}{4}$

E. $\frac{8}{10}$

8. Which fraction is smallest?

A. $\frac{2}{3}$

B. $\frac{4}{5}$

C. $\frac{11}{12}$

D. $\frac{2}{5}$

E. $\frac{1}{2}$

9. Choose the decimal for $\frac{3}{8}$.

A. 0.375

B. 0.4

C. 0.5

D. 0.625

E. 0.875

10. Choose the decimal for $\frac{2}{5}$.

A. 0.4

B. 0.04

C. 0.5

D. 0.6

E. 0.2

11. What is 4 x 4 x 4 in exponential form?

A. 3^4

B. 64

C. 16

D. 4^3

E. 12

12. Find the value of 5 cubed.

A. 555

B. 125

C. 27

D. 25

E. 5

13. Peter entered 9 games and won 8 of them. What is the ratio of the number of games he won to the total number of games?

A. 8 : 7

B. 8 : 10

C. 9 : 1 0

D. 8 : 9

E. 10 : 9

14. What proportion of this grid is shaded?

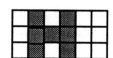

A. 7 : 18

B. 18 : 7

C. 7 : 10

D. 8 : 18

E. 8 : 20

15. Pizza is on sale at Nancy's Pizzeria. You can buy 3 slices of pizza for the price of $2. Which proportion shows how to find the cost of 9 slices?

A. $\frac{2}{3} = \frac{9}{n}$

B. $\frac{3}{2} = \frac{n}{9}$

C. $\frac{2}{5} = \frac{n}{9}$

D. $\frac{3}{2} = \frac{9}{n}$

E. $\frac{3}{5} = \frac{9}{n}$

16. Donna read 7 reports in 9 hours. Which proportion shows how to find the number of reports she can read in 27 hours?

A. $\frac{7}{9} = \frac{n}{27}$

B. $\frac{9}{7} = \frac{n}{27}$

C. $\frac{2}{9} = \frac{n}{27}$

D. $\frac{7}{9} = \frac{n}{30}$

E. $\frac{2}{7} = \frac{n}{30}$

17. Write $\frac{2}{5}$ as a percent.

A. 25%

B. 30%

C. 40%

D. 45%

E. 50%

18. How is $\frac{7}{100}$ expressed as a percent?

A. 700%

B. 70%

C. 77%

D. 7%

E. 0.7%

19. Which is equal to $\frac{3}{4}$?

A. 80%

B. 75%

C. 65%

D. 50%

E. 34%

20. Kathy got 56 out of 100 problems correct on her math test. What percent of the problems did she get correct?

A. 5%

B. 6%

C. 44%

D. 56%

E. 80%

21. Which renames 9% as a decimal?

A. 0.0009

B. 0.009

C. 0.09

D. 0.9

E. 9

22. Carlos earned $500 last month. Twenty percent came from baby sitting. How much money did he make baby sitting?

A. $50

B. $75

C. $100

D. $150

E. $200

23. The graph shows how Maria spent her money over the last month.
If she spent $400, how much did she spend on transportation?

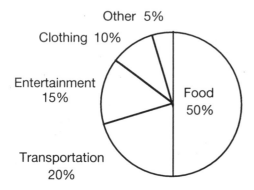

Other 5%
Clothing 10%
Entertainment 15%
Food 50%
Transportation 20%

   A. $200
   B. $140
   C. $100
   D. $90
   E. $80

24. Which line segment is approximately 2 inches long?
   A. ___
   B. _____
   C. _____
   D. _____
   E. _____

25. What unit of length would you use to measure the weight of a bag of sugar?
   A. pint
   B. quart
   C. gram
   D. pound
   E. yard

26. Max bought two tickets to the concert at $11.45 each. How much change did he get from $30?
   A. $7.10
   B. $7.50
   C. $7.90
   D. $8.10
   E. $8.20

27. Julie paid $4.50 for a sandwich and $.80 for a soda. If the tax was $.37, what was the change from $10?
   A. $5.50
   B. $4.70
   C. $4.33
   D. $4.23
   E. $4.13

28. Meg spent 3 hours 20 minutes watching TV. If she started at 4:30, what time did she finish?
   A. 7:30
   B. 7:40
   C. 7:50
   D. 8:00
   E. 8:10

29. Barry got to the gym at 3:45 and left at 6:30. How long was he there?
   A. $2\frac{3}{4}$ hours
   B. $2\frac{1}{2}$ hours
   C. $2\frac{1}{4}$ hours
   D. $1\frac{3}{4}$ hours
   E. $1\frac{1}{2}$ hours

30. Which symbol in the box makes the sentence true?

3/5 ☐ 60%

A. +
B. -
C. =
D. <
E. >

31. Which symbol in the box makes the sentence true?

$2\frac{1}{4}$ ☐ $\frac{10}{4}$

A. x
B. ÷
C. =
D. <
E. >

32. Chris charges $12 for the first hour to mow a lawn. He charges $10 for every hour after the first. Which equation shows how much he charges for 4 hours of mowing?

A. C = 12 + 4 x 10
B. C = 10 + 4 x 12
C. C = 12 x 10 + 4
D. C = 10 + 3 x 12
E. C = 12 + 3 x 10

33. Aliza has 5 quarters and Norma has 2 dimes. Which sentence shows the amount of money Aliza and Norma have together?

A. 5 + 2 = ☐
B. 5 + 25 + 2 + 10 = ____
C. 5 x 25 + 2 x 10 = ____
D. 2 x 25 + 5 x 10 = ____
E. 7 x (25 + 10) = ____

34. Find the value of ☐ if

☐ ÷ 4 = 3 x 3

A. 36
B. 30
C. 24
D. 18
E. 12

35. Which point indicates the ordered pair (2,4)?

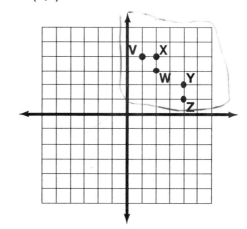

A. X
B. Y
C. Z
D. W
E. V

PART 2

Answer each of the following questions.

36. What are the coordinates of point P?

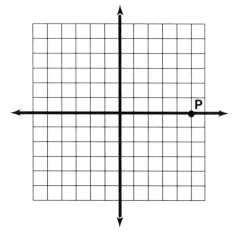

    A. (5,0)
    B. (1,5)
    C. (6,0)
    D. (6,3)
    E. (0,6)

37. What is the missing number?

x	y
2	7
7	12
12	17
18	?
32	37

    A. 20
    B. 21
    C. 22
    D. 23
    E. 24

38. What is the next number that would appear in the series?

40, 33, 26, 19, 12, ____

    A. 9
    B. 8
    C. 7
    D. 6
    E. 5

39. What is the measure of ∠AOD in the figure below?

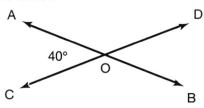

    A. 20°
    B. 30°
    C. 40°
    D. 140°
    E. 180°

40. Estimate the measure of this angle.

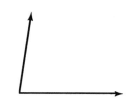

    A. 40°
    B. 80°
    C. 90°
    D. 120°
    E. 150°

41. Which edge is parallel to edge LM?

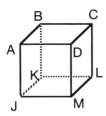

A. $\overline{AB}$

B. $\overline{MJ}$

C. $\overline{BC}$

D. $\overline{KL}$

E. $\overline{AD}$

42. Which segment is perpendicular to $\overline{EF}$?

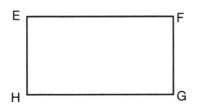

A. $\overline{FG}$

B. $\overline{GH}$

C. $\overline{HE}$

D. $\overline{EG}$

E. $\overline{FH}$

43. Which two shapes are congruent?

A.

B.

C.

D.

E.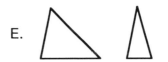

44. Select the pair of sides of the two triangles that are congruent to each other.

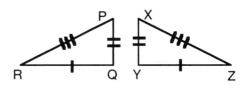

A. $\overline{QR} \cong \overline{XZ}$

B. $\overline{QR} \cong \overline{XY}$

C. $\overline{PQ} \cong \overline{XY}$

D. $\overline{PQ} \cong \overline{YZ}$

E. $\overline{PR} \cong \overline{XY}$

45. What part of the circle is $\overline{AB}$?

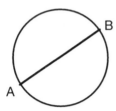

   A. center

   B. radius

   C. diameter

   D. circumference

   E. chord

46. If the diameter of a circle is 120 cm, then how long is the radius?

   A. 10 cm

   B. 20 cm

   C. 30 cm

   D. 60 cm

   E. 80 cm

47. Which figure has 6 faces—all squares?

   A. pyramid

   B. cylinder

   C. sphere

   D. cube

   E. cone

48. How many edges does a rectangular prism have?

   A. 4

   B. 8

   C. 12

   D. 16

   E. 20

49. The perimeter of a square is 40 cm. What is the length of each side of the square?

   A. 5 cm

   B. 10 cm

   C. 12 cm

   D. 15 cm

   E. 20 cm

50. What is the perimeter of a rectangular room whose length is 22 ft and whose width is 15 ft?

   A. 40 ft

   B. 50 ft

   C. 74 ft

   D. 80 ft

   E. 84 ft

51. Find the area of the shaded portion of the diagram. Each square of the grid is a square centimeter.

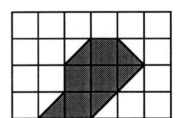

   A. $6\frac{1}{2}$ sq cm

   B. 7 sq cm

   C. $7\frac{1}{2}$ sq cm

   D. 8 sq cm

   E. $8\frac{1}{2}$ sq cm

52. Find the area of this figure.

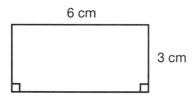

A. 12 square centimeters

B. 14 square centimeters

C. 18 square centimeters

D. 24 square centimeters

E. 30 square centimeters

53. What is the volume of the rectangular prism?

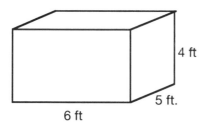

A. 20 cubic feet

B. 60 cubic feet

C. 80 cubic feet

D. 100 cubic feet

E. 120 cubic feet

54. What is the volume of a cube with edges equal to 5 centimeters?

A. 25 cubic centimeters

B. 50 cubic centimeters

C. 75 cubic centimeters

D. 100 cubic centimeters

E. 125 cubic centimeters

55. What is the probability that if you spin the spinner it will stop at the shaded area?

A. $\frac{1}{8}$

B. $\frac{1}{4}$

C. $\frac{3}{8}$

D. $\frac{1}{2}$

E. $\frac{5}{8}$

56. A bag has 10 marbles in it. If 2 marbles are blue, 4 are red, and 4 are yellow, what is the probability that if you pick one marble from bag, it will be blue?

A. $\frac{6}{10}$

B. $\frac{4}{10}$

C. $\frac{3}{10}$

D. $\frac{2}{10}$

E. $\frac{1}{10}$

57. The menu for the Grand Plaza Restaurant shows 4 main courses and 5 desserts. How many combinations of main courses and desserts can be made?

A. 4

B. 5

C. 9

D. 20

E. 25

58. If a penny is tossed 100 times, it is most likely that the number of tails will be
    A. Close to 50
    B. Close to 40
    C. Close to 30
    D. Close to 20
    E. Close to 10

Use this table to answer questions 59 and 60.

Amount of Sale	Tax
$1.00 – 1.07	$.07
1.08 – 1.21	.08
1.22 – 1.35	.09
1.36 – 1.49	.10
1.50 – 1.64	.11
1.65 – 1.78	.12

59. How much is the tax on $1.22?
    A. $.07
    B. $.08
    C. $.09
    D. $.10
    E. None of the above

60. If you paid 11 cents tax on a item purchased, which of the following could be the cost?
    A. 1.05
    B. 1.17
    C. 1.27
    D. 1.39
    E. none of the above

Use this bar graph to answer questions 61 and 62.

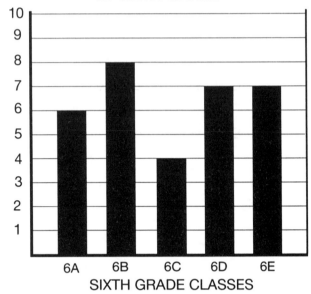

NUMBER OF COMPUTERS IN SIXTH GRADE

61. How many computers does Class 6C have?
    A. 3
    B. 4
    C. 5
    D. 6
    E. 7

62. How many more computers does Class 6E have than Class 6A?
    A. 1
    B. 2
    C. 3
    D. 4
    E. 5

63. Find the mean and the median of these numbers:

    42, 49, 44, 41, 39

    A. Mean: 43   Median: 41
    B. Mean: 43   Median: 42
    C. Mean: 44   Median: 41
    D. Mean: 44   Median: 42
    E. Mean: 42   Median: 43

64. The temperatures at noon in Nick's room during the past week were: 79, 75, 72, 80, 77, 63, and 65. What was the mean temperature for the week?
    A. 69
    B. 70
    C. 71
    D. 72
    E. 73

65. Round 7652 to the nearest 1000.
    A. 7000
    B. 7500
    C. 8000
    D. 8500
    E. 9000

66. Round 37.5 to the nearest whole number.
    A. 35
    B. 37
    C. 38
    D. 39
    E. 40

67. What is the best estimate for 701 x 92?
    A. 63,000
    B. 72,000
    C. 48,000
    D. 6300
    E. 6000

68. Henrik spent 3 hours and 45 minutes on a train going to Chicago to visit a friend. What additional information do you need to find the time he got there?

    A. the length of time he spent with his friend
    B. the time he left on his trip
    C. the time he returned home
    D. the amount of time he stayed in Chicago
    E. the route he took to get there

-121-

69. Dan and Susan cycle towards each other from opposite ends of a cycling trail. Dan cycles at the rate of 9 miles per hour and Susan cycles at 8 miles per hour. If they meet in 3 hours, how long is the trail?

    A. 24 miles

    B. 27 miles

    C. 51 miles

    D. 72 miles

    E. 90 miles

70. Bertha sold 120 magazines at $2.50 each. Which operations would you perform to find out how much more money she must receive before sales reach $500?

    A. add and multiply

    B. multiply and divide

    C. multiply and add

    D. multiply and subtract

    E. divide and subtract